MW01703326

THE DIVINE HEART OF GOD THE FATHER

2nd Revised Edition

Marcelle Bartolo-Abela

All references to Sacred Scripture in this book are taken from *The New Jerusalem Bible* (1999, Stand. ed.). NY: Doubleday.

ISBN 978-0-9837152-9-0

The icon of the Divine Heart of God the Father, part of which is shown on the front cover, was written by Fr. Richard G. Cannuli, O.S.A.

Published by
Apostolate of the Divine Heart
P. O. Box 37
East Longmeadow, MA 01028
Email: adivheart@gmail.com
http://divineheartofgod.wordpress.com

Printed in the United States of America.

DEDICATION

To God the Almighty Father with all my love, adoration, praise thanksgiving and veneration, for graciously deigning to provide me with the subject matter for this book.

- Marcelle Bartolo-Abela

ACKNOWLEDGMENTS

Heartfelt thanks and gratitude to the Blessed Virgin Mary, Archangel Michael and Anthony, for their help with the actual writing of this book.

- Marcelle Bartolo-Abela

DECLARATIONS

Decree

The decree of the Congregation for the Propagation of the Faith, A.A.S.58, 1186 (approved by Pope Paul VI on October 14, 1966) states that the **Nihil Obstat** and **Imprimatur** are no longer required on publications that deal with private revelations, provided that they contain nothing contrary to faith and morals.

His Holiness, Pope Urban VII states:

"In cases which concern private revelations, it is better to believe than not to believe, for if you believe and it is proven true, you will be happy that you have believed because our Holy Mother asked it. If you believe and it should be proven false, you will receive all blessings as if it had been true, because you believed it to be true" (Pope Urban III, 1623-44).

The *Catechism of the Catholic Church* states:

"Throughout the ages, there has been so-called "private revelations," some of which have been recognized by the authority of the Church. They do not belong, however, to the deposit of faith. It is not their role to improve or complete Christ's definite Revelation, but to *help live more fully by it* in a certain period of history. Guided by the magisterium of the church, the sensus fidelium knows how to discern and welcome in these revelations whatever constitutes an authentic call of Christ or of His saints to the Church" (p. 23, #67).

Sacred Scripture states:

"Do not quench the Spirit. Do not despise prophetic utterances. Test everything, retain what is good" (1 Thes. 5:19).

CONTENTS

PART IV - Living In, With, For and Through God the Father

PART V – The Divine Family

PART X - The Reign of God the Father

INTRODUCTION

In this book, a series of brief narratives are provided, that give an intimate portrayal of God the Father in relationship with His adoptive children on earth, together with His Divine Heart Encompassing All Hearts with Infinite Love. In Part I, we are introduced to who God the Father Is and how to develop true intimacy with Him, through our free-will consent to Him as our Father and the union of wills. In Part II, we are given a foretaste of Heaven as the soul rests in the Father, meeting His Divine Light, through the heart of the soul. We are made aware of what is entailed in presenting our souls to our Father, together with the meaning of both the Third Ark and the Father's Covenant, as we are introduced into the manner and process whereby Heaven and earth become joined upon the territory of the soul, in the beginning of the coming of the New Israel.

In Part III, we are introduced to the Divine Heart of God the Father Encompassing All Hearts and His Infinite Love for us, together with the mystical interplay existing between the Divine Heart of God the Father, the Sacred Heart of Jesus, the Immaculate Heart of Mary, the Holy Spirit and the Heart of the Holy Trinity. In Part IV, we learn about the tremendous experience of what it is like to live, in, with, for and through the Father as an adoptive child of God, with particular focus on His Beauty, Love, Order, Peace, Sweetness and Tenderness. Meanwhile, in Part V, we are provided with a brief glimpse of God the Father's Divine Family.

In Part VI, we are shown the manner, process and depth to which we wound God the Father's Divine Heart by our sins, together with the vital necessity of consoling our Father, whereas in part VII, we have a brief overview of the liberating experience of living in the Father's Divine Will. In Part VIII, we are introduced to the process by which we are intimately fused from our souls to the Divine Heart of God the Father, when we re-enter to live in His Infinite Love and Will, whereas in Part IX, we see God the Father on the Cross with His Son. In Part X, we are given an overview of the current state of the world, how we have neglected God the Father both individually and institutionally, together with the imperative need to defend Him and return to Him; as well as a brief introduction into the forthcoming Reign of God the Father, in the Eucharistic Era of the Holy Spirit.

PART I

GOD THE FATHER

1. GOD THE FATHER

Who is God the Father?

God the Father is the supreme Being, the Alpha and the Omega of all creation. Described in the Old Testament as acting, "with faithful love towards thousands of those who love Me and keep My commandments" (Ex 20:2-6), and in the New Testament as, "our Father in heaven" (Mt 6:9), many of us acknowledge that God exists, with many, if not most, of those who believe saying that, "We believe in one God, the Father Almighty, Maker of heaven and earth, and of all things visible and invisible," as professed in the Creed. But to what extent do we really know our Heavenly Father, especially in this post-Christian day and age? That is, on a personal basis despite all our regular, or not-so-regular, professions of faith?

God the Father is the Creator of the entire universe, the Maker of all mankind (Gn 1:1-33, 2:1-25); He is our Father in every sense of the word. As children who are literally the direct product of His handiwork, our Father loves us with infinite love and profoundly desires to be *the* central part of our lives. In fact, our Eternal Father intensely longs for us to develop an intimate relationship with Him: a relationship characterized by the most heartfelt of ongoing conversations of intimate sharing, analogously to the form of relationship that we would normally have with our earthly fathers. Naturally, such conversations with our Divine Father would occur within the context of the epitome of functional child-father relationships. However, why would our Father desire us to develop such intimacy with Him, given that He is the Almighty and Omnipotent God – that is, He certainly does not need us?

God the Father profoundly desires to be present to us, *in* us, with us and for us as Father, throughout the course of our daily lives – as He wants us to reciprocally live in Him, with Him, for Him and through Him – precisely because that is His primary function as God the first Person of the Holy Trinity. He is the Father of everyone and everything that has ever existed, exists and is yet to exist, despite the ongoing and obstinate denial of many regarding such a basic, immutable reality. Our Divine Father created us with a love that we cannot even begin to fathom: love that has to be experienced, in order to start being believed. He created us in order that He could delight in us, as His children, and so that we too could take full pleasure and delight in Him as our Father. All this because, in both essence and fact, we are the human product of His handiwork: that is, we are the only beings on earth with immortal souls and whom our Father decided to create in His own image and likeness (Gn 1:27).

The delight of God the Father in creating human beings as His children rapidly became clouded over, shortly after the outset, by and through the original sin committed by our First Parents (Gn 3:1-24). However, our Father's intense and burning desire to both be with us and in us, enjoying us as His children, never diminished. Indeed, it grew exponentially to the extent that He sent us His only-begotten Son, Jesus Christ, to redeem us in His sight, because our Father did not want any of us to undergo the tortures that we would have had to otherwise pass through, in order for the gateway re-establishing access to our Father to be re-opened (Mk 14:10-72, 15:1-47, 16:1-20). Meanwhile, in our present times, our Father has both been and is becoming increasingly accessible to each and every one of us, in a manner highly reminiscent of His Presence during the Old Testament era. God the Father is proceeding to increase His Presence on earth in this manner for two principal reasons: firstly, because He cannot bear to be separated from us His children any longer, in and through the distance that presently exists between us. Secondly, because the time is now ripe for His Reign to establish itself fully on earth, as we have been asking Him to do, in and through the Lord's Prayer (Mt 6:10), for over two thousand years.

Hence, our Eternal Father has a profound, burning and, to date, un-satiated desire to both directly and intimately share with us everything that occurs, throughout the course of our earthly lives. He yearns to be both with us and in us, everywhere that we are, with a pining and aching Divine Heart, desiring profoundly, with sad longing, to be a vital part of everything we do. In fact, our Father deeply wishes to be *the* central part of our houses, our families, our communities, our societies and our global world, by being loved, adored, praised, worshiped and venerated as our One, True and only Father. God the Father is positively hankering for us to approach and speak with Him regularly as little children, trustingly and lovingly sharing with Him every aspect of our daily lives: our anxieties, aspirations, desires, fears, labors, joys and sorrows; with us carrying out such sharing, with our Heavenly Father, with filial abandonment and trust from the innermost recesses of our hearts. Our Father also desires us to converse with Him not through the intellectually rich, but affectively barren (hence, rather distancing and defensive), language of the scholars or giants of doctrine. He wants us to speak with Him using the simple, colloquial language of little children: the unvarnished language of either untarnished or regained innocence; with genuine intent, simplicity of mind, heartfelt respect, filial love and complete trust in Him, from the very core of our beings.

In sum, therefore, God the Father loves us with infinite and intense love. He profoundly desires that, as His adoptive children, we do not hesitate to welcome Him into our hearts and lives as our One, True Father. Developing an intimate relationship with Him and conversing with Him in a natural manner, so that He can delight in us and we can delight in Him, in a reciprocal, but boundless, circle of divine intimacy and love. We will find that, when we proceed to develop this kind of relationship with God the Father, He never fails to respond to us with profound solicitude, both interiorly – in and through the hearts of our souls (His specific residence in us as His living temples; 2 Co 6:16; St Andrews Productions, 2009) – and exteriorly, through various means. Furthermore, we will find that when we welcome Him as our Father with genuineness and sincerity in our hearts, God the Father both listens and attends to our needs with a gentleness, loving softness, Fatherly tenderness and joy that are incomparable, incomprehensible and inexpressible on a human level: a completely attuned attentiveness that is, in essence, a foreshadowing experience of the fullness of our inheritance (Paul VI, 1964). Such an experience, in fact, occurs through the giving of our free-will consent to the Father, to come and be the central part of our lives, because through this process we open up space for Him to fulfill His Fatherly function to the maximum in our lives, allowing Him to literally inundate us with the profound, felt infinity of His intense love, by both becoming and being willing to accept it.

The aforementioned process of intimate relationship and dialog with our Father, that He so deeply yearns to have with every one of us, directly touches His Divine Heart in its profundity, making God the Father *want* to give us everything that we need and desire (and then some) throughout our daily lives, rather than simply be persuaded to grant them to us out of Mercy. So when we decide to go ahead and welcome our Father into our hearts, with heartfelt genuineness, simplicity and trust of true filial love, we give both our Father and ourselves an immeasurable and inexpressible joy and happiness, because they result in *the* child-Father relationship of Infinite Love. In return for approaching Him in this manner (in deciding to return to live in Him, with Him, for Him and through Him), God the Father generously and benevolently repays our trust in Him and love for Him as Father, by actively showering down upon us an abundance of providence and love far beyond the reach of our wildest dreams, hopes and imagination. All this happens not because we deserve any of it, because we do not, but because our Father has been, Is and will remain, in eternity, *the* Eternal Father of Life, Light and Love.

Developing Intimacy with Our Father

God the Father most intensely yearns to develop true intimacy with us, His children on earth. But many of us choose to remain distant from Him, hesitant and possibly fearful, if not downright cold and indifferent, toward His profound and never-abating interest in us. Others instantly enter into sputtering rants and tirades at the very mention of His holy Name, despite our Father's infinite love for us: a love that we need to experience, to be able to truly start comprehending, in relation to its boundlessness, immensity, profundity and timelessness. In fact, as the only living creatures on earth to possess souls – as the only creatures to have been stamped with the imprint of our Father Himself in the hearts of our souls, at that precise moment of the individual creation of each and every one of us (St Andrews Productions, 2009) – we have, in both essence and fact, been made by God our Father to receive and give love, from and to Himself and others. But throughout the years of our existence as human beings, we have both been and remain, for the most part, unwilling to give back to our Father even just a fraction of His love for us, that He manifests to us constantly without fail.

In reality, we take God the Father's Presence and existence for granted, turning to Him when everyone and everything else fail us, to begrudgingly ask Him for what we have been virtually unable to obtain for ourselves. To all intents and purposes, we treat our Father as though He is a 24/7 department store of earthly desire- and need-fulfillment – going in, asking for and getting what we need, then leaving and 'conveniently' forgetting all about Him, until our next unsatisfied need arises – instead of attempting to develop a true child-Father relationship with Him, with all the give-and-take that such an intimate, familial relationship necessarily entails. Not that our Father does not help us when we ask for His assistance, no matter how ungrateful we may both have been and remain, for God the Father helps us ongoingly in a multitude of ways: ways that we still have great difficulty acknowledging. But as our Father – as our *real* Father – God the first Person desires, without abatement, to be most intimately involved in our lives; living both with and in us, His children, on earth, throughout the mundane course of our daily lives. Our Father wants to become united to us in this manner, because deep, reciprocal knowing constitutes the very essence of the child-Parent relationship – a relationship and familial dynamic all the more needed in our present age, given the physical and/or emotional absence of so many earthly fathers from the lives of their children.

God the Father is the most sweet, gentle, tender, loving, providential and merciful of fathers. He created us to, with Him, form a central part of an intricate dance of knowing, loving, adoring and glorifying, that results in indescribable joy, love, peace and happiness for us, while delighting beyond words His Divine Heart. He wants us all to experience Joy, Peace, Love and Happiness, that can never be provided by anyone on earth, toward the innermost recesses of our souls. Hence, our Father wants us to accept Him, without further reservations, into the depths of our hearts and minds, so that we can fearlessly, intimately and most lovingly share with Him everything that happens in our lives, no matter what the context and content of such may be. In fact, our Father has both requested (St Andrews Productions, 2009) and continues to unceasingly request (Apostolate of the Divine Heart, 2012) that each one of us proceeds to develop this kind of intimate relationship with Him, because He is our One, True Father and we are really His children.

When we muster up sufficient courage to start sharing our lives with our Heavenly Father in this manner, conversing with Him simply, plainly, honestly and intimately in the silence of our hearts, without fear and with complete filial trust, we will find that our Father responds back to us with immeasurable tenderness, literally inundating us with His infinite love, while making available to us everything that we need. Such is the relationship that our Father has both instituted and desires to have with all of His children on earth: that is, the reciprocal intimacy and love of the true child-Father relationship.

Achieving Union with God the Father

God the Father wants us to both pray formally and speak colloquially with Him on a regular (daily) basis, sharing all our joys and sorrows, hopes, needs and desires with Him, so that He can truly be and act as Father, in the earthly course of our lives. But many of us seem to experience difficulty in either communicating or communicating effectively with our Father, especially in the intimate manner that He so deeply desires. Such difficulty generally arises both out of fear and lack of adequate knowledge about who our Father really is, together with lack of true knowledge about how God the Father is when in relationship with us. The fear arises from our stereotypical, albeit highly incorrect, image of our Heavenly Father as a punitive and vengeful God, whereas the lack of adequate knowledge arises from both our historical and current neglect in engaging with our Father, in the true child-Father relationship - both factors that can be easily remedied, through openness on our part.

Our Father is Infinite Love: the sweetest, most tender, gentle, playful and benevolent of fathers. He is immeasurably patient, infinitely wise, ever-present and omnipotently helpful, even when we fall short of His standards (His commandments), which we do regularly and consistently. In desiring familial intimacy with us, our Father is not attempting to needlessly complicate our lives, although He does not dissuade us from doing this, should we prefer to do so. All that He is requesting is that we really start treating Him as our One, True Father: that we speak to Him colloquially throughout our days with *constancy, primacy, centrality, childlike simplicity, genuineness of heart, filial love* and *deep honesty* - in essence, all those qualities that resulted in the passionate worship and friendship of Moses with Yahweh, after the former met the Presence of the latter in the burning bush (Ex 36:8 to 40:35).

It is immaterial what the quality of our communication, our prayer, may have been with God the Father, prior to our developing real intimacy with Him, for when we talk to our Father with the said qualities in our hearts, His Divine Heart becomes so profoundly moved by our puny attempts to please Him, that He descends most rapidly to scoop us up into the boundless confines of His Heart; nesting us closely and safely inside His precious Core, while raining upon us a downpour of His graces, to compensate both for our original and ongoing lack, with, in and through the Alpha and Omega of His Being. In fact, developing an intimate relationship with our Father results in the all-encompassing and -satisfying embrace within the very core of our souls, an experience that remains ongoing as long as we live in His Divine Will, and that is literally felt in every fiber of our beings.

Hence, from the instance we develop our relationship with God the Father, all other attempts at intimately conversing with Him become both possible and relatively easy, falling into place with great naturalness and simplicity; with the entire process of what we can consider as the jigsaw puzzle of prayer (formal and informal) suddenly coming all together, in a comparatively effortless manner. This occurs because the greatest desire of our Father's Divine Heart is to be truly intimate with us as Father, in both essence and fact instituting union with us and even more, so that He can live *in* us while we reciprocally live *in* Him; literally turning us into the earthly arks of the living God (2 Co 6:16), in and through the heart of our souls.

The *Fiat*

Key to achieving union with God the Father is giving our *fiat* to Him: saying our unconditional, freely-chosen "yes" to the desires of His Divine Heart, both when we first decide to develop an intimate relationship with

Him and ongoingly throughout the course of our lives. As Mary said "yes" to the Archangel Gabriel when he announced to Her that She would bear the Son of God despite being a virgin (Lk 1:26-38), within the context of knowing fully that She could be stoned to death for Her decision; and Jesus said "yes" to God the Father right through Gethsemane, His Passion and Crucifixion; similarly are we all called, insistently, by our Father to give Him our wholehearted "yes," so that we can both enter into and live in His Divine Heart and Will, the confines of Infinite Love. Our "yes" to the Almighty Father, in fact, commences or re-commences our journey on the path to holiness (a universal call open to everyone; Paul VI, 1964), personally and effectively empowering us to contribute to restoring order in our global disorder, while simultaneously facilitating the full coming of our Father's Reign on earth – the Glorious (Eucharistic) Reign, in the era of the Spirit – by entering into and starting to live in the descent from Heaven of the New Israel (the New Jerusalem; Bartolo-Abela, 2011; Is 35:1-10, 51:3-11, 60:1-22, 62:1-12, 65:17-25, 66:10-24; Rv 3:10-12, 14:1, 21:1-4, 21:10-27, 22:1-5).

Naturally, giving our unconditional *fiat* to God the Father, does not mean that we will suffer as Jesus Christ and the Virgin Mary did, or that we will even be called to martyrdom (red or white martyrdom respectively) as They were, for none who came, are and have yet to come, will ever come close to going through what They did, during Their lives on earth. Although some of us may, indeed, be called to endure persecution and/or martyrdom in the forthcoming days, for the glory of the Father (Bartolo-Abela, 2011; Congregation for the Doctrine of the Faith, 2000; Dn 8:24-25, Rv 2:10-11, 3:10, 6:9-11, 11:7-10), prior to the re-chaining of Satan and his minions in the abyss (Rv 20:1-6) by Our Lady and St Michael, followed by the full establishment of Our Father's Reign on earth. Thus, saying "yes" to our Father largely means freely and deliberately intertwining our wills with His Divine Will, preferring His Desires over ours, to re-enter to live in the all-encompassing embrace of His Divine Heart.

When we unite ourselves with God the Father in this manner, especially if if achieve such unity through formal consecration to Him (Apostolate of the Divine Heart, 2012; St Andrews Productions, 2009), we become fully His property. Then, our Father most graciously and benevolently deigns to come and dwell in the heart of our souls, through the Holy Spirit, uniting us even more firmly to Him, by spiritually fusing the heart of our souls to the Core of His Divine Heart. We start finding ourselves regularly meeting our Father's Presence in the heart of our souls, as the Divine Light (Lossky, 1997), while starting to live in the beginning of the coming of the New Israel, the prime characteristics of which are the peace, love, joy and happiness of Heaven. Our Father's glory starts penetrating everything we do, causing both ourselves and our actions to serve as ever-growing beacons of light, that manifest the way Home to as-yet distant others, amid the dense, continually increasing darkness of our present world (Apostolate of the Divine Heart, 2012; St Andrews Productions, 2009).

The Free-Will Choice

On one side of our lives is God the Father, the Alpha and Omega of the universe, with His infinite Life, Light and Love, together with the peace, joy, hope, love and happiness of Heaven: infinite bliss for eternity. On the other side of our lives is Satan, the prince of the abyss and of this world, with his ceaseless death, darkness and hatred, together with the lies, betrayal, anguish, hopelessness, despair, conflict and torment of Hell: infinite, unimaginable damnation and torture for eternity. In the midst of our lives is the territory of our own free will: that territory which is generally pressured by various agents, external and internal, turning it into a veritable battleground of decision-making, in relation to the fate of our eternal souls, so that we do not cave in to the path of least resistance. But despite all rationalizations of 'attenuating circumstances' that many, if not most, of us like to ever so diligently come up with, on having to make a decision, it is vital to remember that *our wills can never be overridden without our express consent* – not even under circumstances entailing the pressure of extreme coercion. For, in both essence and fact, we still retain the freedom to choose what our actions and behaviors shall be – we retain free will – even in the severest of circumstances, unless we are seriously mentally challenged.

Given such an immutable and universal reality, therefore, whom are we going to choose to live with, throughout the course of our earthly lives: God the Father or Satan? Every time we do not actively unite our wills with that of our Father, *by default* we end up uniting them with the will of Satan, even though we may believe otherwise, because when we decide to meet what the world desires *on its own terms,* we essentially serve as Satan's mini-agents on earth, since he is the ruler of this world. Being 'in the middle of the road' does not exist, no matter how much we may fool ourselves into believing otherwise (under the rationalization of being 'reasonable'), because, in essence, we are either living internally to our Father's Divine Will or we are not; it is as simple as that. In the latter case, given that we are not 'for Him,' we are either by default or deliberately 'against Him,' despite our ceaseless arguing in this respect.

So we need to start deeply reflecting on the vital issue of whom are we going stand with, live with and live for, in the course of our earthly lives, because at stake is the fate of our immortal souls. We need to seriously consider the spiritual consequences of each and every one of our choices, from within the structure of the aforementioned context, to make truly informed choices about our eternal fate. For the choice of both the present and the future is solely ours: it depends uniquely upon our own free wills (except for minors), and many of us know very well that we will ultimately only reap that which we have sown.

The Union of Wills

God the Father desires that each of us joins their will to His Divine Will, to freely and voluntarily open up space for Him to function fully as our Father, in every moment of our lives. This has been, is and will remain the predominant desire of His Divine Heart: a desire present before He created first man and woman. But, some may ask, how can we effectively do this? Or others may ask, what would result from uniting our wills to our Father's Will?

Uniting our wills to our Father's Divine Will, is both the manner and process through which we enter to live in the confines of His Divine Heart: His infinite love and the beginning of the coming of the New Israel (Apostolate of the Divine Heart, 2012; Rv 21:2). We consent that our Father comes to live not solely with us but *in* us, in the heart of our souls (St Andrews Productions, 2009), while raising us up to actively live in Him, with Him, for Him and through Him. But given that our Father is indeed the Almighty, why do we need to bother to give Him our consent, in uniting our wills with His, so that He can come to reside in us? Cannot He just go ahead and do all of the above by Himself?

Certainly! Our Father can to do everything on His own, given His Omnipotence, but as Father rather than Master, He chooses not to do so, because He regards us truly as His adoptive children (with free intellects and wills) rather than slaves. So God the Father neither overrides nor retracts from us our free wills, despite the pain, sorrow, grief and considerable anguish we ongoingly cause Him, through our constant misuse of such a gift. Instead, He openly manifests to us the desires of His Divine Heart, His innermost longings, hungrily and thirstily pleading with us, like a veritable beggar, for genuine filial love and reciprocity, on the doorsteps of our hearts. Our beautiful Father respects the choices we make, despite the erroneousness of most of our choices; in reality, He never gives up on us. He has both pleaded and continues to untiringly plead with us to return to His Divine Embrace, because we are truly His children and He wants us to enjoy each other for eternity.

PART II

MEETING GOD THE FATHER

2. MEETING GOD THE FATHER

A Foretaste of Heaven

As human beings presently living down here on earth, most of us have become habituated to the daily humdrum of our lives. We wake up in the morning, salute our family if we have one, then proceed to get ready and go about our daily duties. In the evening or late afternoon, we generally have dinner, then firmly plant ourselves in front of the television, internet, or both simultaneously, while attempting to spend some time with family and/or friends. After that we proceed to wind down and withdraw for the night, only to return to largely the same routine throughout many of the days of our lives. Such a *laissez-faire* attitude, in fact, seems to characterize the lives of many of us, with said *laissez-faire*-ness becoming even more pronounced in the domain of our spirituality.

Many, if not most, of us tend to consider ourselves lucky if we manage to drag our feet through the gates of Heaven, by doing the least possible we can do toward this aim, throughout the course of our granted lifetime on earth. Many of us think that we will automatically spend a period of time (short or not-so-short) in Purgatory after our death, since we consider that only a literal handful ever really stand the chance of entering directly into the Kingdom of God the Father: both the Kingdom and Presence of God that are *the* part of our adoptive inheritance. Thus, since so many of us think about our eventual destinies in this unreflective manner, why should we bother bettering ourselves spiritually, given that we would ultimately reach our desired destination, albeit with detours and delays – some of them quite unpleasant – along the way? Why should we become and live as truly spiritual beings, in the course of our daily lives?

The aforementioned *laissez-faire* attitude is not reflective of what we have been called to be, in our lifetime on earth, because our spiritual calling – regardless of our societal and other statuses – has always been, is and will remain to become saints. In fact, it was during His ever-famous sermon on the mount that Jesus Himself told us with certainty, "be you therefore perfect, as also your Heavenly Father is perfect" (Mt 5:48); while God the Father Himself told the Israelites, "be holy, for I, Yahweh your God, am holy" (Lv 19:2); calls both echoed and renewed all throughout the universal call to holiness (Paul VI, 1964). But how many of us really stop to deeply ponder upon the inherent nature and process of this fundamental reality? Rather than simply accede to the mistaken notion that we need to take all these words with a larger-than-normal pinch of salt? Especially, since most of us seem to consider the attainment of perfection, thus holiness, almost impossible to achieve?

How many of us, especially in this day and age, tend to consider as saints those people found "out there in books," rather than considering as saints people who have lived or are living in our midst, if not possibly being some of our very own selves? Can we, as mere human beings, experience an ongoing foretaste of Heaven while still alive, since we are living in the domain of exile of time and space? Yes, we can indeed experience ongoing foretastes of Heaven while still living down here on earth, despite the strong disbelief of some of us and the relentless denial of others. We can freely, voluntarily and deliberately give ourselves to God the Father, consenting fully that He graciously deign to descend to live in us and with us, filling us with Himself – His Presence and Divine Light – in the heart of our souls.

The Heart of the Soul

Within the deepest recesses of a soul is a place that has been created by God the Father; this place can only be accessed by Himself as First Person of the Holy Trinity. At the moment of our conception, right at the beginning of our cellular development as human beings, the said place within the soul beholds for a split-second the fullness of Life, Light and Love who is its Creator: the Being of our Heavenly Father (St Andrews Productions, 2009). The process occurs before the said core in the soul becomes shut down through original sin, and then re-shut down through all the other sins we commit after baptism, if the latter has taken place. This place of deepest recess in our souls is the heart of the soul.

It is through the profundity and indelibility of this imprint by God the Father, upon the heart of the soul, at the moment of the latter's creation, that as human beings we are inherently and ongoingly homesick for our true Home, despite the resistance and denial of so many of us, in both acknowledging and opening ourselves up to this simple, fundamental reality. As human beings, made in the image and likeness of God (Gn 1:26-27), we are unable to experience true rest, peace, love, joy and happiness – the peace, love, joy and happiness of Heaven – until we voluntarily allow our souls to return back to their Father, to be lovingly held and cradled in, by and through His all-fulfilling and glorifying Embrace. We were made *by* and *for* our Creator, yet we search for respite everywhere except from Him. Thus, our souls are inherently restless, even though we may be unaware of this, because they are continually in a state of relentless searching until they can meet their Father and Creator anew, in the fullness of His Life, Light and Love.

But since most of us are rather far from being saints in our lives and spiritual journeys, is it possible, some may ask, for us to give our souls to God the Father, so that He can reopen the heart of our souls while we are still living down here on earth? Thus, in essence and fact, consenting and asking our Father to descend to live in us, in and through the heart of our souls; enabling us to live in Him, with Him, for Him and through Him in turn, for the rest of our lives? It is both possible and relatively easy to give our souls to our Father, so that He can reopen their heart to the delightful intimacy of His Presence and Light. We can achieve this by genuinely re-purifying and re-dedicating our souls to God the Father, through a formal process of purification and consecration to Him (e.g., St Andrews Productions, 2009). This process of re-purification and re-dedication to God the Father, results in our becoming earthly arks – living temples – of the living God, with our Father reciprocally serving for us as *the* Ark Himself.

All we need to do is to decide to turn our faces toward Him – even if we initially do this timidly, hesitatingly and, possibly, even somewhat fearfully – with genuineness of intent in our hearts and minds, asking Him with simplicity, faith and filial trust to accept us back into His Divine Heart. This, in essence, telling our Father that we truly desire to be His children from this moment onward, that we really desire Him to become an intimate part of our daily lives. For simplicity, genuineness and sincerity of heart never fail to bring God the Father rushing out to meet us with boundless joy and delight, in a manner analogous, but not limited, to that of the father of the famous prodigal son (Lk 15:11-32): descending most rapidly to fill the entirety of our beings with His infinite Life, Light and Love; in and through the re-opened heart of our souls. In fact, such genuine turning of our faces to Him is the only thing that our Heavenly Father really expects from us, to swiftly come and live with us and in us, as Father. But unless we actively ask our Father for this gift, He will not come to us, continuing to wait patiently on the sidelines of our lives, until we finally make our request to Him, because unlike the dark prince of this world, our Father never violates the domain of our free-will.

Resting in God the Father

Only in God the Father can we ever experience true rest, the complete fulfillment of all our innermost needs and desires, including those that we are presently unaware of, because it is our Father who is the Alpha and

Omega of all creation, including our own selves. But for us to start achieving even the inklings of such fulfillment, we need to become true children of God, by deliberately choosing to enter into and live ongoingly in His Divine Heart and Will. No one and nothing else on earth, no matter how intimate or profound any of such experiences or relationships may be, can or will ever approximate the relationship of intimacy with our Heavenly Father; a relationship of intimate fusion. Only the Creator Himself can fully satisfy the most deeply hidden and craven needs of our beings and souls. Thus, if we really desire to live, while still living here on earth – if we want to live life fully, rather than simply exist – we have to choose to return to live in, with, through and for God the Father, because absent our consent, our Father will not force upon us the deepest desires of His Divine Heart, despite His most intense longings and yearnings for us. That is the predominant desire of God: that every human being on earth finally acknowledges Him as the One, True and only Father, choosing deliberately to return to live in His Divine Heart and Will: the divine embrace of Infinite Life and Love.

Meeting the Divine Light

When a soul meets God the Father in the heart of her soul, after He has re-purified her, made her fully His by sealing her with His kiss of Infinite Love, then benevolently deigned to descend into His ark, the soul becomes instantly awestruck at the profundity, splendor and majesty of our Father's beauty. No earthly comparison or vocabulary exists to effectively describe and do adequate justice to our Father's Glory: it is, in essence, a foretaste of the Beatific Vision that constitutes meeting the Divine Light (Lossky, 1997). The sheer immensity, intensity and infinity of Life, Light and Love that our Father Is, leaves the soul firmly glued to His Presence, no matter how much she may attempt to detach herself from Him, and despite the fact that our Father's Presence is still veiled.

The soul becomes highly unwilling to do anything but remain there, interiorly transfixed, to continue gazing upon and adoring God the Father in all His might and Glory. Words and songs of love, praise, thanksgiving, veneration and worship, start independently and incessantly arising from the innermost core of the soul, being offered up to God as a heartfelt gift of deep reverence and praise. This is a gift that is regarded by our Father as priceless, because it is given to Him spontaneously by the soul of one of His creatures on earth: an adopted child. Meanwhile, throughout the entire process, the soul achieves full recognition and acknowledgement of the Omnipotence of the Father as Creator, thoroughly embracing His

Presence, within the heart of her soul, as her Almighty, Eternal and Heavenly Father.

Upon meeting our beloved Father in this manner, all the needs and wants of the soul vanish, as she becomes completely saturated and satiated in and through His Presence: a foretaste of that reality of eschatological fullness that is the Father's Divine Life in, with and through Jesus Christ (Apostolate of the Divine Heart, 2012; Paul VI, 1964). The infinite peace, joy, love and happiness of Heaven fully envelop every fiber of the soul's being, and the soul starts virtually perceiving the world around her through a new set of eyes and ears. In fact, the soul starts seeing, hearing and understanding things that occur throughout the course of daily life from within the prism of our Almighty Father's Presence, leading her to want to live in Him, with Him, for Him and through Him in everything she does, rather than simply being in union with Him.

This happens because, at the precise moment that God the Father decides to descend to live in the heart of a soul, after re-purification and re-dedication to Him, in both essence and fact the soul no longer lives separately from our Father but fused with Him and to Him, specifically from the heart of the soul itself to the Core of our Father's Divine Heart. Consequently, this process leads the soul to live in, with, for and through our Father, in an ongoing relationship of boundless intimacy, love and communication, through the binding power of the Holy Spirit. The soul then proceeds to meet the other members of the Divine Family who are Jesus, the Holy Spirit and Mary, to start similarly developing intimate relationships with them and truly partake in our Father's Family Life as an adopted child of God. All of the aforementioned is just a brief description, of the process of the beginning of coming of the New Israel (Rv 3:10-12, 21:1-7, 21:9-23, 22:1-5).

Presenting the Soul to Our Father

When we present our soul to God the Father, after having freely and deliberately consented to give ourselves to Him, we find ourselves kneeling before His infinite Majesty, facing Him with the soul on the palms of our uplifted hands. The Alpha and Omega sits regally on His throne, facing us in immense splendor and Omnipotence, while Jesus Christ stands closely to His right and the Virgin Mary standing next to Jesus in turn. God the Father, Jesus and Mary all look at us patiently, silently, but most intently, while awaiting the handing over of our soul to God the Father, so that it may become fully His property. Our Father radiates a most luminous and indescribable, veiled beauty that both extends and envelops all surroundings. Our soul resembles a clear orb of light that we hold up, humbly and supplicatingly, both in front of, and to, our Father with our hands. The degree of clarity, luminosity and reflectivity of the orb, that is our soul, manifests the extent to which we have been successful in re-purifying our soul from the darkness of sin, through the combined effort of grace and receptivity to our Father's grace, including the specific graces of reconciliation, re-purification and re-dedication to Him, through formal consecration.

We then proceed to bow profoundly to His Majesty, approaching slowly on our knees toward the steps of the Throne upon which our Almighty Father resides. With courage, humble trust and filial love in our hearts and minds, we then lift up our eyes to gaze directly upon our Heavenly Father, while stretching out our uplifted hands with the orb of our soul on them, to give to Him for safekeeping and tending. Our Father benignly, but none-the-less majestically, arises from His Throne and graciously descends the steps of the latter to meet us, taking both to Himself that clear orb of light, faith, trust and hope that is our soul. As we continue kneeling there with our uplifted faces, gazing with unearthly stillness upon our Father's Light and Beauty, God the Father then proceeds to slowly ascend back upon His throne, while very tenderly and lovingly tucking away the orb of the soul closely into His left side, to preserve it with great vigilance and joy by His loving Presence. The above is a brief, but actual, description of what it is like to give our souls to God the Father, through formal consecration to Him, highlighting what it is like to become a truly adopted child of God, in a union of fusion not found elsewhere.

The Third Ark

Upon consenting to give ourselves to God the Father, we become His living arks, His little temples, on earth (2 Co 6:16), while our Father becomes *the* Ark Himself. But what is, in essence, the Third Ark? An ark is both the residence of the Presence of God and His haven of rest, among His people on earth; reciprocally providing the latter with the Father's undying Light and unfailing guidance, to shepherd them effectively to safety. A physical example of the ark was that of Noah with whom the Father established His first covenant (Gn 6:18, 9:9-17), after having commanded him to build and enter into the ark with members of all types of species, so that these would be safeguarded from the global purification of the earth through the Deluge (Gn 6:5-22, 7:1-23). In fact, Noah and his family remained safe throughout the entire purification of the earth at the time, despite all the fear they experienced at the latter destroying all iniquities and other people present.

So having elucidated the concept of the ark, we can see how through the instrumentality of the First Ark of God the Father, both Moses and Aaron safely and effectively shepherded the people of Israel (God's first-born children; Ex 4:22) through all the pain, suffering and bloodshed of the first Passover and exodus from Egyptian slavery. Our Father shepherded them safely throughout the desert of Sinai, where His covenant with Noah was ratified through the Decalogue, until the Israelites reached the Promised Land (Jos 1:1-5). In fact, in the Old Testament, we see numerous instances of the Ark of the Covenant – the residence and haven of the Presence of God – going regularly in front of the Israelites, in order to open up the battle-lines for them, so that they could achieve victory.

Meanwhile, through the instrumentality of the Second Ark of the Virgin Mary (CCC 2676; Rv 12:1-2) from whom Jesus Christ was born through the overshadowing of the Holy Spirit, Jesus effectively shepherded the new People of God (CCC 781; Paul VI, 1964; Rv 5:9-10) through the pain, suffering and bloodshed of the second Passover and the exodus of all mankind from spiritual slavery. All through the desert way from Cana, through Calvary, to Golgotha where God the Father established His new and everlasting Covenant with us (CCC 1612; Lk. 22:20) through the Lamb's Crucifixion and Death, to re-open for us the gate through which we could access that promised land of the fullness of our inheritance (Paul VI, 1964). Neither in this instance did our Father remove His people from the world, but through both His Son and Mary, as the residence and haven of both God and all mankind (Jn 19:26-27), He protected them from the Evil One (Jn 17:15): a protection and shepherding that continue to this day.

Through the instrumentality of the Third Ark which is the Seal of God the Father for our souls (Rv 3:10-12), our Almighty Father – through, with and in the redemptive Sacrifice of Jesus Christ, the co-redemptive haven of Mary's Immaculate Heart, and the binding unity of the Holy Spirit – is, in both essence and fact, effectively shepherding all His children through the pain, suffering and bloodshed of the third Passover and exodus from the spiritual slavery of our times. All through the desert way of neo-paganism, the abomination of desolation and global purification of the earth from its present iniquities (Dn 8 & 9, 11 & 12; Rv. 6 to 9, 11, 13 & 14, 16 & 18), to the promised land of both the individual and collective coming of the New Israel (Rv 3, 21-22); together with the giving of the new name (Rv 2:17, 21:3-4) to the children of God. As has occurred historically, all of the above has started happening under our eyes while we remain on the face of the earth, with one of the entries into the Third Ark being through consecration to God the Father.

The Covenant of God the Father

At the time of the First Ark, God the Father established His long-lasting covenant with the people of Israel, making them His chosen people – a "kingdom of priests, a holy nation" (Ex 19:6) – insofar as they were prepared to obey Him and keep His covenant (Ex 19:5). Our Father did this so that Israel could serve as both the city of His rest and delight, since they were the firstborn of all His children on earth. Meanwhile, at the time of the Second Ark, God the Father ratified, broadened and perpetuated His covenant into the new and everlasting Covenant with the People of God (Paul VI, 1964); making them His "chosen race, a kingdom of priests, a holy nation, a people to be a personal possession" (1 P 2:9), insofar as they maintained His commandments (Jn 15:10). This happened so that our Father could once again find both rest and delight among His new firstborn, selected through their own spiritual desires to find and live with Him and for Him, from among all His children on earth: both Jews and Gentiles.

Now, at the time of the Third Ark, God the Father is again ratifying, further broadening and perpetuating His everlasting Covenant with all those of His children who truly desire to live in Him, with Him, for Him and through Him as their One, True and only Father, in both essence and fact gathering "every nation and every language" (Is 66:18), to revitalize His chosen people taken from both the First and Second Arks through "descendants from Jacob . . . [and] heirs to My mountains from Judah" (Is 65:9). He is giving them the sign (Is 66:19), that is the new name (Is 65:15; Rv 2:17) of "God-within-them" (Rv 21:3), in and through His Fatherly Seal for their souls (Rv 3:10-12). The Almighty Father is revitalizing the people into the ones that are "redeemed to be the first-fruits for God and for the Lamb . . . [because] no lie was found in their mouths and no fault can be found in them" (Rv 14:4-5). Some of these our Father will "make into priests and Levites" (Is 66:21), causing them to lead His revitalized, re-Christianized people to become "the Holy People . . . 'Sought-after,' 'City-not-forsaken'" (Is 62:12) that will serve as the Father's "holy city, the New Jerusalem coming down out of Heaven" (Rv 21:2). In this our Heavenly Father will find full delight, glory and rest by living in, among and through His children (Rv 21:3) "until the thousand years had passed" (Rv 20:3), as His Kingdom comes down on earth in fulfillment of our ongoing request to Him through the Lord's Prayer (Mt 6:10). Consequently, we will experience an ever-increasing foretaste of the fullness of our inheritance (Paul VI, 1964), resulting in our living in, with, for and through the most Holy Trinity, in the Reign of God the Father on earth, during the era of peace of the Holy Spirit.

The Joining of Heaven and Earth: Beginning of the New Israel

Immeasurable, boundless and verbally indescribable are the peace, love, joy and happiness of Heaven - the Peace, Love, Joy and Happiness of God the Father, that He is so generously and benevolently offering to all His children in these post-Christian times: namely, to those who freely and deliberately select to enter to live, in the confines of His Divine Heart. For, upon entering to live in our Father's Heart, we enter to live in His Divine Will – Infinite Love, literally joining together Heaven and earth on the territory of the heart of our souls. Such joining of Heaven earth is, in fact, the individual fulfillment of our oft-repeated request to the Heavenly Father in the Lord's Prayer, "Your Kingdom come, Your Will be done on earth as is in Heaven" (Mt 6:10), because when we genuinely and fully give ourselves to our Father through consecration to His Divine Heart, God the Father most joyously and delightedly descends to live in the heart of our souls, initiating the full establishment of the New Israel (Rv 21:2).

PART III

THE DIVINE HEART OF GOD THE FATHER ENCOMPASSING ALL HEARTS

3. THE DIVINE HEART OF GOD THE FATHER ENCOMPASSING ALL HEARTS

Entering Into Our Father's Divine Heart

The main keys to entering into the Divine Heart of God the Father are childlike simplicity and filial trust, because since our Father is the Benevolent Almighty, He will provide us with everything we need, at the moment we need it, in order to live effectively in His Heart and Will, and it will never cause us spiritual harm. A related key to entering into our Father's Heart is genuine willingness to do our best in abandoning ourselves completely in our Father's Hands, despite both the fear of so many to do so and the fact that such dependence grates directly against the grain of our individual natures and collective cultures. Other keys to entering to live in our Father's Divine Heart is to approach Him with sincere intent of heart and mind, ready to embrace His Will as manifested to us in the short-term – on a daily basis, regardless of what this may entail. All this despite the fact that our Father's Divine Will may, and oftentimes does, appear to go directly contrary to our own will and fly completely in the face of 'reason;' within the additional context of not knowing concretely what will happen to us in the long-term. Such are the main keys to entering, remaining and living in our Father's Divine Heart, the aforementioned process giving a brief illustration of how we both become and remain true children of the Father.

The Disposition of Our Hearts

To what extent do we genuinely possess Love – the very Presence of God the Father – in the heart of our souls? To what degree do we sincerely have true love in our hearts: the love which is both reciprocal and reciprocates Infinite Love? To what extent are we ready, at any given moment, during the course of our daily lives, to set aside the incessantly demanding and noisy desires of our selves, in order to truly live out love as our Father's children? And to what degree do we daily come up with rationalizations of all kinds, in order to do our utmost precisely not to live out love?

Many, if not most, of us quite often proudly and loudly proclaim that we love God. Some even like to go about publicly manifesting such a claim in a manner that can be considered analogous to that originally employed by the renowned Pharisee (Lk 18:10-14). However, when it comes down to the wire, to what extent do we truly love our Divine Father in our hearts? To what degree are we both disposed and ready, in the core of our beings, to put our money where our mouths are, in those plentiful, decisive moments when our Father decides to test the sentiments truly contained in our hearts? Are we lustfully desirous of greedily receiving our Father's love, while refusing to love Him according to the desires of His Divine Heart? Do we solely take, but not reciprocate, His Love, in and through the maximum degree of love that we are capable of giving at a specific moment to Himself and others, and not a fraction less? Or do we continue holding something for ourselves in reserve? Giving anything less than our best is, in fact, false – not true – love, despite our endless reasoning and rationalizations, in order to delude ourselves into believing otherwise.

The dispositions of our hearts, therefore, toward Infinite Love are crucial in fulfilling the greatest commandment of all (Ex 20:2-11, Mt 22:37-38): that of loving God the Father with the entirety of our beings – our minds, hearts, bodies, souls and spirits; for it is from such dispositions that our thoughts, intents and actions consequently arise. But how many of us continually attempt to silence our consciences, by rationalizing away all of the above under the generalized, albeit quite familiar, protestation that "if I could, I would but (insert your most preferred lie)?" Thus, how many of us proceed with our daily lives as though nothing we are doing is wrong, or seriously lacking, in some dimension or another toward our Heavenly Father?

It is high time for us to stop, step back and take a deep, thorough look at ourselves, specifically at our heartfelt sentiments, for the dispositions in our hearts determine our true natures, regardless of what we may think or claim in this regard. Only after we genuinely decide to forego the habitual darkness of loving our selves first, can the Life, Light and Love of our Father's Heart descend to live in the heart of our souls, because the infinite Light Who Is God the Father cannot, indeed will not, enter to reside where habitual darkness lives.

Waiting in the Third Ark

Patiently, our Father waits with the Ark of His Divine Heart lovingly offered to us and our souls in His Hands: that Ark which will lead us safely to the haven of Peace, through the Third Passover that constitutes the trials and tribulations of our times. However, despite the door to the Ark of our Father's Heart being wide open for all and sundry to enter into, only a few truly desire to come in, for most either do not care or quite simply do not want to know. Some think that it is not yet time, that there is still plenty of time left, whereas others think that none of this is true, that there exists no such thing as the Ark. Meanwhile, pleading and begging, both with and as Infinite Love, our Almighty Father does not stop calling us to return to Him; since His most profound, predominant desire is to carry us all safely and securely into the heavenly peace of the New Israel, the beginning of the coming of which has already commenced (Apostolate of the Divine Heart, 2012).

Are We Ready?

Are we ready to glorify God the Father, with the entireties of our minds, hearts, bodies and souls, when the moment arrives of the individual testing of both our fidelity and faith? Or are we going to glorify him who has desired nothing but our ruin in every way, since the beginning of time (Gn 3:1-21)? Are we going to both passionately become and be true adoptive children of the Father, or are we going to sit back and be passively lukewarm in our faith: a lukewarmness that will result, without fail, in the eternal loss of our souls (Rv 3:16)?

Are we going to be and act as true members of the Church Militant, believing and proclaiming fearlessly, *"Quis ut Deus?!"* at the critical moment of choice? Effectively helping to chain Satan back into the abyss (Rv 20:1-3) with Archangel Michael (Rv 20:2-3) and the Virgin Mary (Rv 12:1), through Jesus (Rv 19:19-21) and the power of the Holy Spirit, so that the Reign of the Father can finally ensue fully on earth? Or are we going to become known eternally as the cowardly and traitorous Judases of our times? The free-will choice is indeed ours to make, for our Father never imposes His Divine Will upon us, no matter how profoundly and intensely He yearns for us, to return to live in the infinite love of His Divine Heart. Hence, it is time to ponder without further delay: what is the choice that each one of us, individually, is going to make?

Quis ut Deus? Serviam!

"Who Is like God?! I will serve!" This is the victorious cry first uttered by Archangel Michael (hence his name), after defending God the Father against Lucifer and the principalities and powers who rose up against Him, before the beginning of time (Rv 12:7-9). It is precisely this cry which needs to be our wholehearted, immediate response to our Father, when He asks whether we will cooperate with Him in His Divine plan, for both ourselves and all humanity. We do not any need money to say "yes" because our Father will provide us with everything we need, in order to fulfill His desires. All we need is a sincere heart and good will (Lk 2:14), to unite our will to His and start bringing His Kingdom down on earth, together with heavenly peace, into our severely troubled world.

The Divine Heart of God the Father Encompassing All Hearts

The Divine Heart of God the Father is the visually concrete, symbolic representation of the infinite love our Father both Is and has, for all the hearts of mankind, in His bosom: precisely that place where our Father profoundly desires to, parentally and paternally, hold and nurture each one of us on earth (Apostolate of the Divine Heart, 2012). The specific perspective of the Divine Heart is that of our Father resting on His side, while both looking down on and making known, in a tangible way, the profundity and intensity of His love toward all humanity. Below is a grayscale reproduction of the original pencil drawing of the Divine Heart of God the Father Encompassing All Hearts (with) Infinite Love, whereas overleaf are grayscale reproductions of the actual diptych icon (based on the pencil drawing) of the Divine Heart, as written by Fr. Richard G. Cannuli, O.S.A.

Left-hand side of the diptych, ecumenical, revealed icon showing the Divine Heart of God the Father Encompassing All Hearts: Infinite Love.

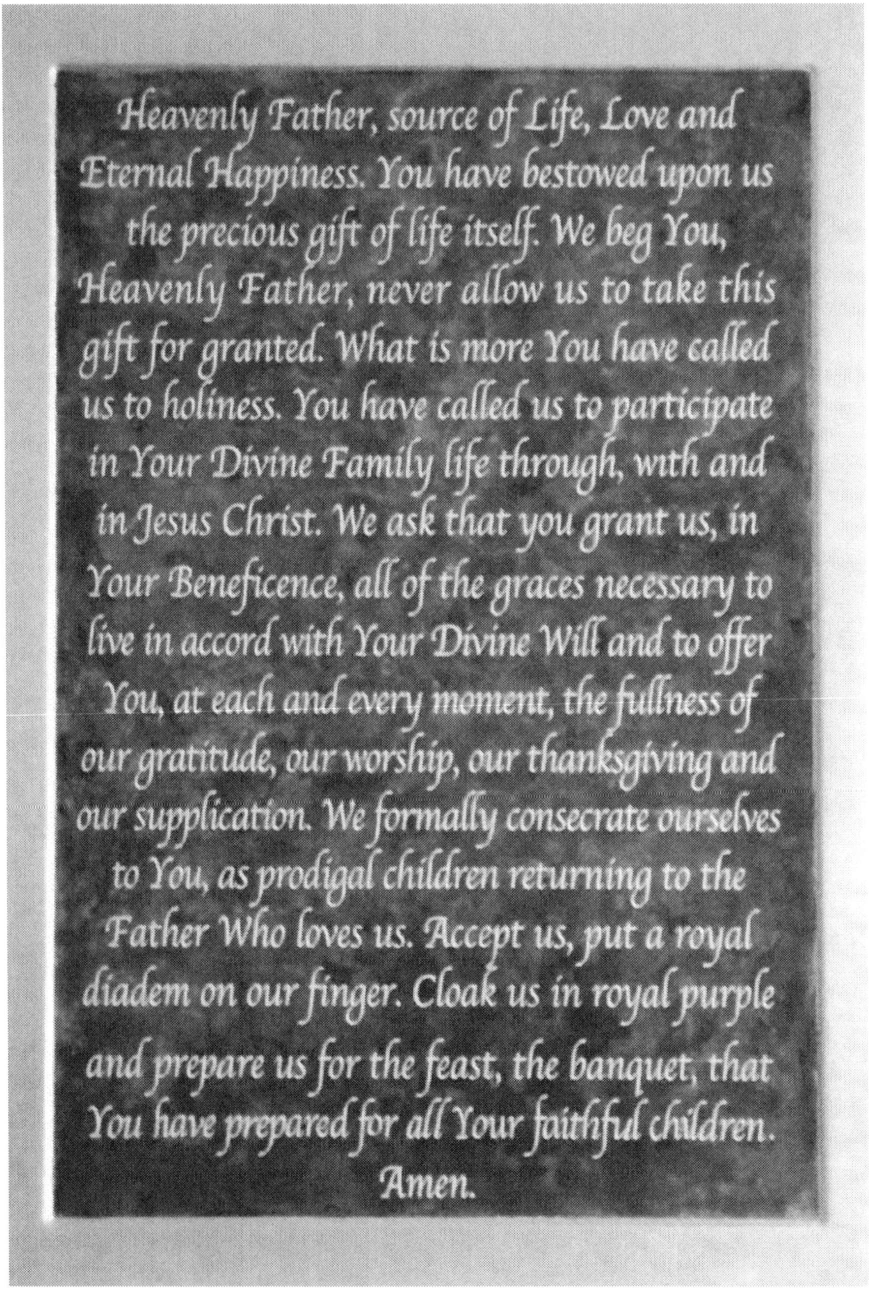

Right-hand side of the actual diptych, ecumenical, revealed icon of the Divine Heart, showing the Consecration (Seal) Prayer to God the Father.

The small heart encircled with thorns, enclosed in the right upper region of God the Father's Divine Heart, is the representation of (1) the Core of our Father's Heart, (2) the Sacred Heart of Jesus; and (3) the Heart of the Holy Trinity. For it is (a) the very heart of the Father's Divine Heart, (b) the place where "the only begotten Son . . . [lives] in the bosom of the Father" (Jn 1:18); and (c) the place from which the Holy Spirit – the spirit of the Spirit Who Is God – issues forth. Meanwhile, the brilliant, radiant sun within which the Divine Heart of God the Father is embedded represents both God the Father as the Life, Light and Love (the Creator and Sustenance) of the world, as well as the Holy Spirit Himself.

The Core of the Father's Divine Heart

The Core of the Divine Heart of God the Father is that place, in our Father's Heart, from where issues forth the spiritual umbilical cord of Life, Light and Love; connecting itself, directly and unfailingly, to the heart of the soul, after the latter has been re-purified and re-dedicated, to become a temple of the Living God. Such is the manner in which the souls of mankind become spiritually attached to our Heavenly Father, when we decide to return, to live in the loving embrace of His Divine Will, because it is from the Core of our Father's Divine Heart that the water of Life incessantly streams forth, for us to drink; so that we can experience and live within the invisible, but omnipresent, structure of the Presence of God, in the core of our beings.

The Core of our Father's Heart is beautiful beyond any possible verbal description – it has to be seen to be believed – and It is (1) One with, (2) encompasses; and is (3) analogous to the Sacred Heart of Jesus; while also encompassing the hearts of all mankind. Because the Core of our Father's Heart is the very origin of Life, Light and Love; given that He is the Alpha and Omega; His Core is also the Heart of the most Holy Trinity. It is precisely from our Father's Core that His Thought, Word (Jn 1:1) and Holy Spirit originate (Gn 1:1-2; the spirit of the Spirit Who Is God emerges), in order to bind Jesus, Mary, the whole heavenly court and all human beings who are in a state of sanctifying grace, to God our Almighty Father. Meanwhile, it is both at and through the Core of our Father's Heart that, at the very instance preceding the physical conception of a human being but overlapping into it, the soul becomes stamped in its heart with our Father's image and likeness, before it is shut down by original sin. This is the manner in which our newly formed souls behold their Divine Creator in His Trinitarian Glory, at the moment of our creation (St Andrews Productions, 2009).

Thus it is that the soul, having been struck, at its very heart, with the unequalled brilliance and glory of the One, True Father, in its earthly life it becomes unable to find true peace, joy, life, light, love and happiness, until it re-encounters the Father in the confines of His Divine Heart. Indeed, our souls constantly seek to be safely held in our Father's Embrace, despite our generalized unawareness of this or outright denial of its presence. Interiorly we are in a state of ongoing restlessness that manifests itself externally in various ways, until we decide to return back to our Father and Creator; regardless of how much we may try to silence such restlessness of soul, through all kinds of exterior means. Let us, therefore, not hesitate any further in reuniting ourselves with our true Origin, so that we can satiate ourselves fully with Life, Light and Love directly from that unceasingly streaming fountain that emanates from the Core of the Divine Heart of God the Father, through the Sacred Heart of Jesus, in the binding unity of the Holy Spirit.

The Source of Life, Light and Love

God the Father Is Life, Light and Love Himself. Ever-ready to welcome us into His bosom – the Core of His Divine Heart – where His only-begotten Son, Jesus, resides, our Father waits patiently for our return: the return Home of the prodigal children to their Father (Lk 15:11-32; Apostolate of the Divine Heart, 2012; St Andrews Productions, 2009). But many of us, sadly, neither desire to know Him as Father, nor even want to get to know Him. This infinitely loving, tender, immeasurably sweet, kind, wild, firm, gentle, humorous, patient, very playful, benevolent and adventurous Father of ours is rejected, more than anyone else in His whole Kingdom, precisely because He is the Almighty: the Alpha and Omega of the universe. Many are afraid of Him, whereas others recoil at the mention of His very Name. Others simply do not want to know Him, while even more others ruthlessly desire Him to be obliterated with totality from the face of the earth.

Our Father is not a vengeful God, although at times He can, indeed, become angry as all genuine parents do, at the endless wrongs that we have no problem committing; especially when we perpetrate, and continue to unhesitatingly perpetrate, such wrongs toward the most vulnerable of His creatures. God the Father is Infinite Love. Thus, He cannot tolerate our ceaseless injustices in the face of our lack of remorse and repentance. In all honesty, we need to ask ourselves what kind of a Father would God be, if He did not react to what we do, given what we continually inflict on others. But our beloved Father never reacts to us in accord with our human notion of a proportional response, otherwise He would have wiped us off the face of the earth ages ago, since almost everything we do is fundamentally out of lust, gluttony, envy and pride (Bartolo-Abela, 2011).

God the Father is Love; unsurpassable by anything or anyone else. As a Father, He is immensely tender and sweet, firm but extremely loving, with a sense of adventure and playfulness that make even the most mundane occurrences of our lives become wild with excitement, happiness and joy, whenever we open up space for Him to be present in them. Why do we not, therefore, decide to set aside our own prejudices toward Him once and for all – incorrect prejudices born out of both ignorance and other prejudices and biases in turn – to give our Father the chance of taking over the reins of our lives? Hence, accepting Him as a central part of our beings, in effect asking Him to come and live with and in us, in the heart of our souls. When we do the latter, our Father will come to us without fail, because this is the kind of intimacy He profoundly desires to have with every one of us. It is the relationship, in fact, that He had originally envisaged prior to the beginning of time, whereby He would live in, with, for and through us His adoptive children, as we would reciprocally live in, with, for and through our Father.

We will inevitably find that, when we follow His direction and allow Him such prominence and centrality in our lives as Father, we will never again experience a dull moment. For we will, literally, both live in our Father (insofar as is humanly possible while still on earth) and He will live in us, in the heart of our souls. We will start experiencing regularly the fullness of Happiness, which is the happiness of Heaven, that is part of our adoptive inheritance (Paul VI, 1964). Such is the beginning of the fulfillment of God the Father's promise to us, that He will come and live on earth with us as He does in Heaven, in essence and fact commencing the coming of His Reign of Peace. But one caveat exists for the said process to be fulfilled: we need to ask our Father to come and live both in us and among us, in and through the heart of our souls, otherwise He will not come. He will stay on the sidelines of our lives, waiting for our request to be made, and this because He respects our free-will.

The Unity of the Divine and Sacred Hearts

God the Father leads us to Jesus, similarly to the manner in which Jesus leads us to our Father. In fact, Jesus said that, "everyone whom the Father gives Me will come to Me" (Jn 6:37) and that, "no one can come to Me unless drawn by the Father who sent Me" (Jn 6:44). So not only does

Jesus lead us without fail to our Father, as most of us are already aware of, but for those who may go directly to the Father, they will find that they will be inevitably led back by our Father Himself to Jesus; to be raised up in accord with the latter's words, "those whom You took from the world to give Me. They were Yours and You gave them to Me" (Jn 17:6) and that, "No one can come to the Father except through Me" (Jn 14:6).

Such a process of return occurs because we cannot be in the Divine Heart of God the Father without simultaneously being in the Sacred Heart of Jesus, because the Core of our Father's Divine Heart is One with the Sacred Heart of the Son, in and through the unity of the Holy Spirit, since "the Father and I are one" (Jn 10:30), "the Father is in Me and I am in the Father" (Jn 10:38, 14:11); and "Father, You are in Me and I am in You" (Jn 17:21). It is precisely to reconcile us with our Heavenly Father – to re-open the gate for us, in order to be able to return, to live in our Father's Divine Heart and Will: Infinite Love – that Jesus came on earth to redeem us more than two thousand years ago. This is an immutable fact clearly illustrated in the Gospel of John, whereby Jesus both points us toward and shows us the Face and Will of our Eternal Father (Jn 12:44-50).

The Infinite Love of God the Father's Divine Heart

The Divine Heart of God the Father contains within it Infinite Love and Mercy for us His children, despite our considerable frailty which leads us to repeatedly fall through sin, possibly even through mortal sin, greatly wounding His most tender Heart. Mortal sin, in fact, permanently separates us both from our Father and His Presence, unless we reconcile ourselves to Him, through His Sacrament, with sincerity of heart, because it eliminates the Life and Light from our souls, by eradicating sanctifying grace.

The Core of our Father's Heart is indefatigable in calling out to each and every one of us, attempting to reach us in the stubborn hardness of our hearts and minds, in order to sweetly and lovingly coax us to return back to Him, to live in His Divine Will; no matter what the present state of our souls may be. However, despite such coaxing with infinite love – calling and coaxing unfathomable by human standards – many of God the Father's children remain deeply entrenched in sin during this post-Christian age, preferring such a situation, rather than truly loving themselves by taking adequate care of their souls. Others still do not know our Father, do not care to know Him, or actively hate Him; with the latter two preferring the death of their souls so readily inflicted by Satan and his minions (many have bought into the lie that this is pleasurable and edifying), rather than welcoming into themselves the eternal and irreplaceable Love Who Is our One, True and Only Father.

The infinite love that our Father possesses for us, in His Divine Heart, is the very fabric that constitutes the life of our own internal lives, despite our obstinate and ongoing denial of this. Hence, God the Father never stops to actively pursue us in a highly concerned, parental and paternal manner, in order to plead with and beg us to genuinely reconcile ourselves with Him. So that He can restore us to full communion with Himself, (hence eternal Life) in His own Spirit Who Is the Holy Spirit.

A God Madly in Love

Our Father is a God who is madly in love with us: a love that needs to be intimately and fully experienced, in order to be believed. But many of us either experience difficulty comprehending this, or deliberately continue to refuse to understand such a fundamental reality. Not only did our Father, in essence, crucify part of Himself more than two thousand years ago, in and through the person of His Son, Jesus Christ, in order to redeem us from our ancestral Fall and reconcile us with Himself. Now our Eternal Father is generously and benevolently deigning to descend directly Himself, from His Heavenly Kingdom, to literally show us the rapid and deep palpitations of infinite love and tenderness, that He has for us, in His Divine Heart. Let us not, therefore, wound such love any further, by continuing to refuse to return to live in His Divine Will: the Will of His ever-loving Heart.

The Balm of Our Father's Heart

Infinite love is *the* defining characteristic of the Divine Heart of God the Father, because the Triune God *Is* the fullness of Love, despite all protestations to the contrary. Love that is so indescribably limpid, pure, soothing and sweet; so complete in its fullness that it serves as sorely needed balm, for and upon our presently abused souls. Many of us have both injured and continue injuring our souls, without hesitation, through the repeated commission of all kinds of sins on a daily or even more frequent basis, not caring what we have done or continue doing, as long as we satisfy ourselves and our egos in the present moment. We have become superlatively good at attending to every aspect of our exterior lives, at the specific expense of our interior life. But such gross neglect of our spiritual welfare on our part, is a welfare for which we carry personal responsibility in the eyes of God subsequent to attaining full capacity for reason. Our Father has never abandoned or forgotten us. He keeps on chasing us, even in these days of generalized defiance, rebellion, coldness, indifference and active hatred toward Him; especially, we should note, in these days. Our Almighty Father is doing this so that He can completely heal our seriously wounded souls and interiors with the life-restoring balm of infinite love, in and through the Mercy of His most Divine Heart.

PART IV

LIVING IN, WITH, FOR AND THROUGH GOD THE FATHER

4. LIVING IN, FOR, WITH AND THROUGH GOD THE FATHER

Being the Father's Child: the Joy of Being Little

God the Father loves souls who are little, because it is when we become little, both with Him and others, that we open up space for Him to carry out fully His function as Father, in our daily lives. Letting His Majesty, Glory and greatness appear, without hindrance from ourselves or at least a minimum of hindrance, when we become anew like children. However, becoming, being and remaining little is not easy to achieve, because it goes directly against the grain of everything we have been socialized into believing and being since childhood, in our post-Christian societies.

Specifically, many of us are taught that we need to be winners, irrespective of the cost involved in such a process, both for ourselves and others; otherwise, we will be regarded as losers in the eyes of the world. However, we cannot be winners in this sense of the term, if we truly want God to live in us on a daily basis, as such a set of heart and mind only makes our Father shun us in disgust and His Holy Spirit flee, while we virtually force Jesus to re-experience the pain of His Passion and Crucifixion, when we proceed to receive Him in the Eucharist in such a state. We need to be in the world but not of the world, because we cannot belong both to the world and to God, even though many erroneously think that we can have our cake and it eat - a veritable fallacy.

We need to choose, through our own free-will, in whose camp we really wish to live and belong, for if we sincerely desire to gain access to the fullness of our inheritance who Is the Triune God (Paul VI, 1964), by returning to live in the Divine Heart and Will of God the Father, we need to seriously set aside our egos and our selves, to become and remain little for the rest of our lives. The littlest of the little, in fact, so that we can be winners in essence, rather than in name only. Like that our Father becomes attracted to us by our humility and decides that He is, indeed, going to come and live in the hearts of our souls, rather than simply being with us during the mundane routines of our daily lives. When we become little in such a manner, our Father inundates us with His felt Love, Peace, Joy and Happiness: the love, peace, joy and happiness of Heaven, which are incomparable to anything one may experience on earth. Moreover, the freedom and liberty that accompany our becoming and being little can never be matched by the so-called freedom and liberty provided by mankind. Only in littleness can we ever hope and be truly joyful and happy, regardless of what the world may think of us and our choices, because only in littleness can we intimately come to know and live in God the Father. We were conceived by Him to be for Him, since prior to the beginning of time. But for many of us this is the hardest thing to achieve, although by no means impossible, because it represents and is the epitome of counter-culturalness.

Serving as the Living Ark of the Covenant

When we voluntarily and deliberately consent to give ourselves to God the Father, through our own free-will, in essence and fact we become the little, living arks of the Living God, changing the intrinsic nature of our relationship with Him, from one of being simply a member of the People of God (Paul VI, 1964) to one of being truly an adoptive child of God. During the Old Testament era, our Heavenly Father actively dwelt on earth among the Israelites, in the Ark of the Covenant: "I will dwell among the sons of Israel and I will be their God" (Ex. 29:45). Now during this period of our present time that is the end of times described in the New Testament era, our Father is once again returning to dwell on earth by descending into the arks of the Covenant, that is the heart of our souls, when we consent to open our hearts and minds to Him and His Presence. Hence, He is starting to fulfill, on an individual-by-individual basis, the prophecy that "here God lives among human beings. He will make His home among them; they will be His people and He will be their God" (Rv. 21:1-2). For after giving ourselves to Him through formal purification and consecration to Him, the heart of our souls is re-opened by the Father, through His Holy Spirit, to make it anew the indwelling residence for our Father's Presence. This is the manner in which the New Israel is descending from Heaven to earth.

The Need for Filial Trust

How often do we abandon ourselves in our Father's Hands and Will, with the entireties of our minds, hearts, bodies and souls, not knowing, in fact, what the short-term outcome of such filial abandonment will be? That is, the abandonment inherent in and characteristic of the true simplicity and filial trust of a child, in the infinitely loving, immeasurably tender, protectively vigilant and benevolent Father. A childlike abandonment,

Word and Spirit

Coming to Terms with the Charismatic Movement

Alison J. Sherrington

Third edition 2011

Foreword by Rev Dr Geoff Waugh

Published by Philip House
in association with Renewal Journal Publications

Brisbane, Australia

ISBN-13: 978-1466250437
ISBN-10: 1466250437

Printed by CreateSpace, Charleston, SC, USA, 2011

Published by Philip House
www.philiphouse.org

Philip House

in association with

Renewal Journal Publications
www.renewaljournal.com

Renewal Journal

Brisbane, Australia

Contents

Foreword

Alison Sherrington's *Word and Spirit: Coming to Terms with the Charismatic Movement* "is intended as an encouragement to be both faithful to the Word and open to the Spirit."

Her book provides an excellent introduction to contemporary concerns raised by charismatic renewal. It rejects a false dichotomy between Word and Spirit, places experience under the scrutiny of revealed theology, acknowledges a dynamic exegesis which refuses to be contained within our Western conceptual framework (for the wind blows where it will), and explores spiritual gifts in terms of God's sovereign presence in all of life – not merely as theories confined to our paltry categories.

As a comment on faith and obedience, the book calls for courageous openness to God's work in His world in the power of His Spirit. This involves change for us all, no matter what our pet categories may be. God's ways cannot be confined to ours. We are encouraged to seek the Giver even more than His gifts. He is Lord. He gives *charis* (grace) and *charismata* (gifts of grace) more liberally and more comprehensively than any evangelical or pentecostal theology can categorize.

Alison Sherrington affirms the importance of both Word and Spirit and challenges any dividing or emasculating of them. She does not attempt an exhaustive exegesis, but calls for faith in God founded on obedience to the Word of God empowered by obedience to the Spirit of God.

This book is useful as a guide for those confused by the legalism of much current debate (on all sides) because it affirms the primacy of God's Word revealed and interpreted by His Spirit.

Dr Paul Pillai, former Hindu lawyer and the founder of Indian Inland Mission, with a Bible college of 600 students – the largest in India – uses Alison Sherrington's book as an important textbook. He wrote: "The Lord is using this book in a wonderful way. It is one of the most needed books for all of us moving in the Spirit. The Lord used you much to clear many things concerning His ways."

I pray that God will indeed use this book in your life to clarify and apply His Word to you in the power of His Spirit.

Rev Dr Geoff Waugh
Editor, *Renewal Journal*
www.renewaljournal.com

Experiences of the Holy Spirit

The charismatic claims

According to the 2001 edition of the *World Christian Encyclopedia* (D. B. Barrett, G. T. Kurian, T. M. Johnson, University Press, Oxford), in 1970 the number of pentecostal or charismatic Christians throughout the world was 72.2 million, 6.4% of all Christians; in 1995 the number had grown to 477.3 million, 26.9% of all Christians; and by 2000 it had grown to 523.7 million, 27.7% of all Christians (vol. 1, 20). Nearly all pentecostal and charismatic Christians claim they have had an experience of the Holy Spirit which they refer to most commonly as being baptized with the Spirit, being baptized in the Spirit, being filled with the Spirit, or receiving the Spirit. Whatever the expression used (there are several other expressions also) and whatever the variations in the experience of different people, it is evident from numerous testimonies that God's power and love and His empowerment have been felt in an immediate, intimate way.

It is noteworthy that some of these Christians claim to have had this experience of the Spirit at the time of their conversion to Christ, or immediately afterwards, while others claim that they were committed Christians with a saving faith in Jesus Christ as their personal Lord and Saviour for some time – perhaps even many years – before they experienced the Holy Spirit in this special way. Most, but not all, claim that during or shortly after this experience they found themselves speaking words which did not belong to any language known to them. Some say they have had this experience only once, while others claim to have had it on two or more occasions. Some say it came in answer to prayer, with or without laying on of hands, while others say it came unbidden. Some were alone at the time, while for others it was a group experience. Some claim that they experienced sensations of warmth or bright light or torrents of water or an electric current, or even supernatural wind or fire. Others say that although they felt spiritually overwhelmed, they can recall no extraordinary phenomena. However, all these Christians seem to be united in their testimony that this experience has brought them much spiritual benefit, both in their personal lives and in their ability to share with others the Good News of Jesus Christ. Particularly is this true of those who were born again a fairly long time before their personal experience of the Spirit, and who can therefore compare their life in Christ before it with their life in Christ after it.

Does experience matter?

At this point something must be said about the place of experience in the Christian life. The familiar (and perhaps unjustified) criticism that charismatic beliefs are based on experience instead of on Scripture implies that Christians should ignore experience. Even if this were desirable, in practice it is impossible. Every Christian, whether he realizes it or not, interprets Scripture partly in the light of his own experience; and a Christian's interpretation of Scripture largely determines which kinds of experiences he considers valid. In many circles it is acceptable to give an emotional account of a dramatic experience of conversion to Christ, but unacceptable even to mention the possibility that a Christian of our time could have a direct experience of the Holy Spirit.

Since Jesus Christ is Lord of the whole of life, and the Bible is God's Word written by inspiration of the Holy Spirit, the Christian cannot afford either to ignore experience or to base doctrine upon it. Instead, he must try to bring it under the Lordship of Christ by testing and interpreting it as objectively as possible in the light of Scripture while seeking the guidance of the Holy Spirit. Experience that has no Biblical basis must be rejected as false or purely subjective, whereas experience for which there is Biblical support may give the believer a deeper personal assurance of his faith. Although it is Scripture, not experience, that is authoritative for faith and life, Scripture and experience go hand in hand in healthy Christian living, for on different levels each confirms the other. It is interesting to note that many charismatics assert that their experience of the Holy Spirit has brought Scripture alive for them in an amazing way.

The stumbling-block of terminology

One approach which tends to sidestep any serious examination of charismatic claims is to criticize as "unbiblical" the theological terms used by charismatics; for example, Paul's assertion in 1 Corinthians 12:13 that "we were all baptized by one Spirit into one body" is seized upon as "proof" that every Christian was baptized with the Spirit at the time of his conversion (whether or not he was aware of this baptism) and that charismatic claims are therefore unworthy of consideration. Some critics even maintain that the noun form "baptism with the Holy Spirit" is unbiblical; yet if Jesus baptizes with the Spirit, as the Scriptures proclaim (e.g., John 1:33 and Acts 1:5), there must be such a thing as a Spirit-baptism! (The Bible nowhere uses the term "Trinity" either, but theologians find it indispensable.) Criticism of terminology tends merely to avoid the issue of whether there is a major spiritual blessing that many sincere and committed Christians do not seem to have experienced.

Let us for the time being put aside all argumentation about what theological terms should be used to describe experiences of the Holy Spirit such as charismatics claim to have had, and let us first consider whether there is Biblical support for the experiences themselves.

Are there Scriptural parallels?

In Acts there are several examples of direct experiences of the Spirit, each one a little different from the others.

The experience of Cornelius and his group came at the time of their conversion to Christ (10:44-48), while the Samaritans' was some time after their conversion and baptism (8:12-17). The apostles, Cornelius and his group, and the Ephesian "disciples" found themselves speaking words which did not belong to any language known to them (2:4-11; 10:45-46; 19:6), but it is not recorded that the Samaritans and Saul did so when they initially experienced the Spirit (8:17-18; 9:17-18). The apostles, and perhaps some other believers with them, had a powerful experience of the Spirit on at least two occasions (2:1-4; 4:31). The apostles' second experience was in answer to prayer (4:31), and the Samaritans' in answer to prayer with laying on of hands (8:15-17), but the experience of Cornelius and his group came unbidden (10:44). Saul's experience was individual, while the other examples in Acts are of group experiences. The apostles experienced supernatural wind and fire, and later on, supernatural earthquake (2:2-3; 4:31), but no such extraordinary phenomena are recorded in the other examples.

One is forced to admit that there do seem to be parallels in Scripture for the various personal experiences of the Spirit that different charismatics claim to have had.

Is there Biblical support for experiences today?

Some Christians are not convinced that there is Biblical support for direct experiences of the Spirit today, despite the fact that there seem to be parallels for them in Scripture. They take the view that at Pentecost the twelve apostles (and perhaps some other believers) experienced the Holy Spirit on behalf of the whole Church for all time to come, and they therefore regard with the utmost suspicion any suggestion that Christians today may have immediate, intimate experiences of the Spirit. They justify the later Samaritan and Gentile experiences recorded in Acts 8 and 10 in terms of the necessity for Samaritan and Gentile missions to be fully validated in the eyes of the church in Jerusalem; and Saul's dramatic experience of physical healing and spiritual empowerment when the scales fell from his eyes (Acts 9:17-20) is explained in terms of his special calling to apostleship.

It is important to realize that there does not seem to be any Scriptural support for the view that, within the Christian era, direct experiences of the Holy Spirit were to be solely the prerogative of a favoured few in the early days of the Church, and are therefore not available today. Such a view is based mainly on theological speculation concerning exactly what was accomplished in the coming of the Spirit on the apostles at Pentecost. It is true that the first groups of Samaritan and Gentile Christians would have had to experience the Spirit unmistakably, and in the presence of an apostle, for the sake of the complete validation of missions to Samaritans and Gentiles; but can we assume that they otherwise would have had no direct experience of the Spirit, or that they were among only a very favoured few who had such an experience? The weight of evidence is against such assumptions.

If the apostles' experience of the Spirit at Pentecost was on behalf of the whole church for all time to come, why did the apostles themselves need to have that further powerful experience recorded in Acts 4:31? And since the Spirit had already been experienced by groups of Jews, Samaritans (part-Jews), and Gentiles, who together represented the whole of mankind, why did the twelve Ephesian "disciples" of Acts 19 need to have a similar experience when Paul laid his hands on them? It is doubtful whether God's sole purpose in granting them this experience was in order that Luke, the writer of Acts, could use this incident to show that Paul's ministry here was parallel with that of Peter and John among the Samaritans in Acts 8!

Regardless of whether, at the time when Paul found them, the Ephesian "disciples" were Christians or merely followers of John the Baptist, Paul's first question to them, "Did you receive the Holy Spirit when [or after (NIV footnote)] you believed?" (19:2) strongly implies the following: (a) at least at first, Paul took them to be Christians; (b) "receiving the Holy Spirit" denotes an experience that one is aware of; (c) it is possible for Christians not to have had this experience of the Spirit – as we already know from the Samaritans' conversion (Acts 8), and as is also suggested by Paul's own three-day wait after the Damascus road incident (Acts 9); and (d) it is desirable for Christians to have this experience of the Spirit. It is highly probable that in Paul's first question there is also the further implication that it was usual for Christians of his time to have such an experience, whether it came at or after conversion. Paul's meeting with the Ephesian "disciples" climaxed in their experience of the Spirit, which did not come, however, till during or after their baptism (Acts 19:5-6).

The Biblical evidence strongly suggests that, among any number of direct experiences of the Spirit which Luke could have chosen to record, he has selected those which best serve the purposes of his narrative of the expansion of the Church from Jerusalem to Rome.

Far from limiting immediate experience of the Holy Spirit to a favoured few, Pentecost seems to have signified, among other things, the beginning of the availability of such experience to all believers, irrespective of sex, age, and rank. How different from Old Testament times, when such experiences were the prerogative of very specially favoured people, mainly prophets, priests, or kings! In order to explain the Pentecost experience of the apostles, which seemed to some onlookers like drunkenness, Peter was inspired to quote from Joel's prophecy: "In the last days, God says, I will pour out my Spirit on all people" (Acts 2:17); and in view of the later, similar experiences recorded in Acts, Peter could not have been claiming that the whole and final and only fulfilment of this prophecy took place on the day of Pentecost. Since "the last days" will not end until the return of Christ, there is no reason whatsoever to assume that ordinary Christians today cannot experience the Spirit in a way that is akin to the experience of the apostles at Pentecost.

Are modern experiences of the Spirit genuine?

It has been established not only that there are Scriptural parallels for experiences claimed by modern charismatics, but also that there is Biblical support for the availability today of experiences akin to that of the apostles at Pentecost. Nevertheless some Christians, without any Biblical justification, try to restrict the possibility of immediate experiences of the Holy Spirit to the time of the apostles and are reluctant to regard as genuine any more modern experiences of this kind. Their doubts are expressed in such questions as: "Are these people really deceivers, pretending to have had a personal experience of the Holy Spirit in order to appear to be super-Christians? Are they deceived, imagining experiences that have no objective reality? If their experiences are real, are they from God or from Satan?"

Those who regard charismatics as deceivers seize upon a few well-publicized instances of sinful conduct on the part of certain pentecostal or charismatic leaders. They forget that similarly disgraceful things occur from time to time in more traditional churches, but that these churches often manage to keep such events out of the public media, partly because their image is not as controversial. Moreover, the persecution meted out to charismatics in many churches is certainly no incentive for anyone in those churches to pretend to have had a personal experience of the Spirit!

The allegation that so-called experiences of the Spirit today are merely products of the imagination of highly emotional people is a generalization which cannot be sustained in the face of the wide range of personality types, intellectual and educational levels, and social, cultural, and racial backgrounds within the swelling ranks of pentecostals and charismatics. How can the claims of such men as David du Plessis, Michael Harper, and David Watson be so lightly dismissed? Moreover, the theory that such experiences today are always subjectively manufactured in the imagination of those who desire them fails to take account of the testimonies of those who claim that, although they did not seek such experience, and although, in some cases, they did not even consider that it was available today, yet God graciously granted it to them.

If the experiences claimed by charismatics today had no objective reality, one would not expect them to have objective consequences. However, the vast majority of those charismatics whose experience came later than their conversion are discernibly different in their Christian walk thereafter. Something has happened to them. Is this "something" good or bad? Jesus said, "By their fruit you will recognize them" (Mt. 7:20); and from any unbiased assessment it is obvious that most of them bear better fruit than they did before, particularly in the area of increased power in witnessing for Jesus. Even opponents of the charismatic movement will usually admit that charismatics are very zealous for the Lord. This is an outcome that Satan most certainly would not want!

Those Christians who try to restrict the possibility of direct experiences of the Spirit to the time of the apostles are often ignorant of the fact that claims to such experiences are recorded in association with many of the great revivals in the history of the Church all down the ages. Three examples must suffice, of which the first is familiar to many – the individual experience of John Wesley on 24th May 1738, when his heart was "strangely warmed". Less well-known is the event described thus by A. Skevington Wood in *The History of Christianity* (ed. T. Dowley, Lion Publishing, Sutherland, NSW, 1990, p.449):

On 1 January 1739 a remarkable love feast was held at Fetter Lane in London. There the leaders of the Revival were welded into a fellowship of the Spirit in a way similar to what had happened at Herrnhut in 1727. The Wesleys were present, along with Whitefield and Benjamin Ingham, who was to become an outstanding evangelist among the Moravians. 'About three in the morning, as we were continuing instant in prayer,' John Wesley recorded in his Journal, 'the power of God came mightily upon us insomuch that many cried out for exceeding joy and many fell to the ground. As soon as we were recovered a little from that awe and amazement at the presence of His majesty, we broke out with one voice, "We praise Thee, O God, we acknowledge Thee to be the Lord".' This Pentecost on New Year's Day confirmed that the Awakening had come and launched the campaign of extensive evangelization which sprang from it.

Even more amazing is the event which initiated revival on the island of Timor in the twentieth century, and which is described thus in the Publisher's Foreword to Mel and Nona Tari's book, *The Gentle Breeze of Jesus* (New Leaf Press, Green Forest, Arkansas, 1978, p.6):

The renewal exploded with full force in the Soe church the night of September 26, 1965, when the New Testament phenomena of the Day of Pentecost were repeated – a tornadolike wind, visible fire (which prompted police in their station across the street to set off the fire alarm and summon volunteer firefighters), and numerous conversions as well as infillings with the Holy Spirit, complete with speaking in tongues, including English. By midnight, teams of laymen had been organized to begin spreading the gospel the next day.

The cumulative evidence from Scripture, from Church history, and from the testimony of 524 million Christians around the world today, is very strong. Although one could never assert the genuineness of every claim of an immediate experience of the Spirit, it is beyond reasonable doubt that there is indeed available today a major spiritual blessing which is akin to that granted to the apostles at Pentecost and which many sincere and committed Christians do not seem to have experienced. In view of the weight of the evidence for the genuineness of modern direct experiences of the Holy Spirit, and in view of the rapidly increasing numbers of Christians making this discovery in a personal way, one can no longer either ignore these experiences or maintain that they are not for today.

What are the results of such an experience?

Although at this stage the word "experience" must still be used in order to avoid theological terms, it is important to realize that God does not grant an experience merely for the sake of the experience itself. The experience is meant to produce results, and from the united testimony of Scripture, Church history, and modern charismatic Christians it is evident that the most obvious result of an experience akin to that of the apostles at Pentecost is a loosing of the tongue – principally an empowerment to witness for Jesus Christ, but often an empowerment to speak in tongues also.

Before His ascension Jesus told the apostles: "Stay in the city until you have been clothed with power from on high" (Luke 24:49); "You will receive power when the Holy Spirit comes on you; and you will be my witnesses in Jerusalem, and in all Judea and Samaria, and to the ends of the earth" (Acts 1:8). When, on the day of Pentecost, the apostles "began to speak in other tongues as the Spirit enabled them", the Jews from different parts of the world exclaimed: "We hear them declaring the wonders of God in our own tongues!" (Acts 2:4,11); and Peter spoke of this phenomenon in terms of a fulfilment of Joel's prophecy: "Even on my servants . . . I will pour out my Spirit . . . and they will prophesy" (Acts 2:18). Furthermore, on that day Peter's own inspired preaching of God's message (a form of prophecy) resulted in the conversion of about 3,000 people (Acts 2:41)! His words were God's words because his spirit was completely under the control of the Holy Spirit.

Other Biblical records of immediate experiences of the Spirit support this conclusion that the main purpose of such experiences is to confer upon believers a greater ability to speak forth words from God, not in their own strength but by the power of His Spirit. The chief result of the experience of the apostles and other believers after the arrest and release of Peter and John was that they all "spoke the word of God boldly" (Acts 4:31); Saul, immediately after his experience and baptism, "at once . . . began to preach in the synagogues that Jesus is the Son of God" (Acts 9:20); Cornelius and his group spoke in tongues and praised God (Acts 10:46); and the Ephesian "disciples" "spoke in tongues and prophesied" (Acts 19:6). There is no precise indication of the result of the Samaritans' experience, but it was visible to Simon the Sorcerer, who coveted the ability to bring such a change to people (Acts 8:18-19). Whether or not we are called to preach, we as Christians must "always be prepared to give an answer to everyone who asks [us] to give the reason for the hope that [we] have" (1 Peter 3:15). The amazing growth of the early Church came largely through the oral witness of ordinary believers, as is clear from such passages as Acts 11:19-21.

After direct experiences of the Spirit, believers are often more fully equipped than before to minister to people in various ways, in addition to witnessing for Jesus. Jesus Himself did not begin His ministry till after the Holy Spirit had descended on Him like a dove, and He described this ministry not only as preaching but also as healing and meeting every kind of human need in the power of the Spirit (Luke 3:21-23; 4:18-19). When addressing Cornelius and his group, Peter spoke of "how God anointed Jesus of Nazareth with the Holy Spirit and power, and how he went around doing good and healing all who were under the power of the devil, because God was with him" (Acts 10:38). It is significant that after the release of Peter and John, when the apostles and other believers prayed for great boldness of speech and for healings and miraculous signs and wonders through the name of Jesus, the Lord's response was to grant all of them an empowering experience of the Spirit (Acts 4:29-31); and although at first we are told only that they all "spoke the word of God boldly", we find later that the performance of healings and miracles was not the prerogative of the apostles alone. "Stephen, a man full of God's grace and power, did great wonders and miraculous signs among the people" (Acts 6:8); and Philip the Evangelist did miraculous signs in Samaria (Acts 8:6-7).

Although in the New Testament "grace" (unmerited favour) usually speaks of God's love in sending His Son to save us, it sometimes speaks of God's power bestowed upon believers for the purpose of ministry. "We have different gifts, according to the grace given us", and "each one should use whatever gift he has received to serve others, faithfully administering God's grace in its various forms" (Rom. 12:6; 1 Peter 4:10). Since an immediate experience of the Holy Spirit is primarily for the purpose of empowerment for witness and service, it ordinarily results in an increase in the number of spiritual gifts and/or increased effectiveness in the use of gifts already given. Usually one of the factors is a release from inhibiting traits such as shyness and also from bondages imposed by man-made traditions, for "where the Spirit of the Lord is, there is freedom" (2 Cor. 3:17).

What descriptive terms should be used?

Much misunderstanding has occurred among Christians for many years over terminology relating to experiences of the Spirit. The simple solution would seem to be: to describe such experiences, use any of the terms that the Bible uses. Direct experiences of the Spirit recorded in Acts are described in the following ways:

(a) the apostles (and others?):
"baptized with the Holy Spirit", the Greek for which may also be translated "baptized in the Holy Spirit" (1:5; 11:16); "the Holy Spirit comes on you" (1:8); "filled with the Holy Spirit" (2:4); "I [God] will pour out my Spirit" (2:17,18); "he [Jesus] . . . has poured out what you now see and hear" (2:33);

(b) the apostles and others:
"filled with the Holy Spirit" (4:31);

(c) the Samaritans:
"the Holy Spirit had not yet come upon any", or AV "as yet he was fallen upon none" (8:16); "receive(d) the Holy Spirit" (8:15,17); "the Spirit was given" (8:18);

(d) Saul:
"filled with the Holy Spirit" (9:17);

(e) Cornelius and his group:
"the Holy Spirit came on all", or AV "the Holy Ghost fell on all" (10:44); "the gift of the Holy Spirit had been poured out" (10:45); "received the Holy Spirit" (10:47); "the Holy Spirit came on them as he had come on us", or AV "the Holy Ghost fell on them, as on us" (11:15); "God gave them the same gift as he gave us" (11:17);

(f) the Ephesians:
"receive the Holy Spirit" (19:2); "the Holy Spirit came on them" (19:6).

It is highly unlikely that we are meant to make fine distinctions of meaning among the different expressions, especially since the one event is sometimes described in several ways. However, the descriptions do reveal that what is basically the one experience has an outer and an inner aspect. The outer aspect is expressed in the imagery either of gift-giving or of baptism (for, like water, the Spirit is poured out or falls or comes on people). The inner aspect is expressed in the imagery of receiving or being filled. Clearly, it is with Biblical justification that charismatics today tend to use all of these expressions interchangeably to describe their empowerment by the Holy Spirit. In addition, some describe it as an "anointing" with the Spirit, for the Bible speaks of God anointing Jesus with the Spirit for His ministry (Luke 4:18; Acts 10:38). However, when the Bible speaks of believers receiving an anointing from the Lord, it may not always be referring to an empowerment for ministry (cf. 2 Cor. 1:21 and 1 John 2:20,27).

The freedom with which charismatics describe empowering experiences of the Spirit in any of the terms used for them in the Bible, may unfortunately cause misunderstanding with those who hold different interpretations of certain passages of Scripture. Let us briefly look at some common problems of terminology, always remembering that reality is far more important than terms used to express it.

Baptized with (or in) the Spirit

Some believers are accustomed to thinking of the word "baptism" as always signifying a Christian initiation or beginning, and are therefore offended by the implication that not all Christians have been Spirit-baptized. They fail to understand that charismatics are using the term "Spirit-baptism", not to signify being born of the Spirit (saved), but to signify an experience of the Spirit that initiates one into more fully empowered witness and service. Those who have had more than one such experience usually use this term to refer to their first experience only.

Those who seek to restrict the term "Spirit-baptism" to the time of conversion point out that in Acts it is only the experience of the apostles at Pentecost for which the expression "baptized with the Holy Spirit" is used (1:5; 11:16). But were the apostles born again, in a Christian rather than a pre-Christian sense, *before* Pentecost or *at* Pentecost? They were in a unique historical situation, and it is not possible to be dogmatic on this point, particularly in the light of John's record that on the evening of His resurrection day, Jesus appeared to His disciples and "breathed on them and said, 'Receive the Holy Spirit'" (20:22). There are mysteries here that we cannot fathom. Possibly, the apostles first truly became Christians at Pentecost, but the Bible does not clearly say this. In Acts, Luke is more concerned with that operation of the Spirit which empowers believers for ministry than with that operation by which He brings people to new birth.

One very real problem with trying to use the term "Spirit-baptism" for the new birth is that the expression "baptized with the Holy Spirit" is one of a cluster of closely related images which are used for empowering experiences of the Spirit, regardless of whether they coincided with new birth or not. In Jesus' words to the apostles before His ascension He makes it clear that being baptized with (or in) the Spirit is the same as the Spirit coming on one (Acts 1:4-8); yet this same expression of "coming on" is used not only in relation to Cornelius and his group, whose experience coincided with conversion, but also in relation to the Samaritans and the Ephesian "disciples", whose experiences took place after conversion (Acts 10:44 and 11:15; 8:16; 19:5-6).

When Paul asserts that "we were all baptized by [or with; or in (NIV footnote)] one Spirit into one body" (1 Cor. 12:13), he is obviously referring to some kind of incorporation of Christians into the Body of Christ, some kind of union with Him as part of His Body; but the exact meaning is not clear. The baptism he is referring to could be baptism with water, made effectual by the Holy Spirit; or it could be the new birth, although he would then be using the concept of Spirit-baptism with a different meaning from that in Acts; or, as in Acts, it could be Spirit-baptism in the sense of an empowerment with the Spirit for service. However, in this last case we cannot assume that Paul is asserting that all Christians are Spirit-empowered for service, because by "we . . . all" he may be referring only to himself and the Corinthian Christians, to whom he has already said, "You do not lack any spiritual gift" (1 Cor. 1:7).

In his book *Joy Unspeakable: The Baptism with the Holy Spirit* (Kingsway Publications, Eastbourne, 1984, p.270), D. Martyn Lloyd-Jones points out that the view that equates Spirit-baptism with the new birth has gained ground among evangelicals only within about the last one hundred years; yet in many denominations this view is now enshrined unofficially, and sometimes even officially, as the orthodox view.

In support of this view, Peter's words in Acts 2:38 are often quoted: "Repent and be baptized, every one of you, in the name of Jesus Christ for the forgiveness of your sins. And you will receive the gift of the Holy Spirit." Since Peter uses the term "gift", he was probably referring to empowerment rather than indwelling (cf. Acts 1:4-5). But is the Lord really promising that every Christian will be baptized with the Spirit? Peter goes on to say that "the promise [of the Spirit] is for you and your children and for all who are far off – for all whom the Lord our God will call" (Acts 2:39). However, Lloyd-Jones (*Joy Unspeakable,* pp.170-173) asserts that "all the promises of God are always conditional – invariably", and convincingly argues that "all Peter is saying [in Acts 2:38-39] is this: if you repent and believe on the Lord Jesus Christ you are a candidate for these promises. . . .

You are then in a position to receive the gift that we the apostles have already received." He concludes that "we must never interpret Acts 2:38-39 as teaching that automatically everybody who repents and believes, is baptized with the Holy Spirit."

Faced with the dilemma that in many denominations Spirit-baptism tends to be equated with the new birth, some charismatics whose experience of the Spirit did not come till after their conversion have proposed the theory that they were non-experientially baptized with the Spirit at the time of their conversion, but were not "released in the Spirit" to experience that Spirit-baptism and its full benefits till later on. Although the term "released in the Spirit" is unbiblical, it does express something of that greater freedom and boldness which most Christians have after a direct experience of the Spirit.

Giving and receiving the Spirit

The problem with expressions about the "giving" of the Spirit and "receiving" the Spirit is similar to the problem with "Spirit-baptism". Since Pentecost it is certainly not possible to belong to Christ without also having the Holy Spirit. When Paul says, "If anyone does not have the Spirit of Christ, he does not belong to Christ", the context makes it plain that he is referring to the indwelling of the Spirit (Rom. 8:9-11). It is by His Spirit that Jesus is in us, and we are in Him. Since all Christians have the Holy Spirit indwelling them, how is it possible for some to be "given" the Spirit, or "receive" the Spirit, after conversion? Yet these expressions are used not only in relation to Cornelius and his group, whose empowering experience coincided with conversion, but also in relation to the Samaritans and the Ephesian "disciples", whose experiences took place after conversion (Acts 10:47 and 11:17; 8:15-18; 19:2-6).

It is important to understand that, just as the operations of the Holy Spirit transcend human logic, so too do the expressions for them. One may have the Spirit, in the sense of being indwelt by the Spirit, without having been "given", or having "received", the Spirit; and this is merely because in Acts Luke specifically relates these latter expressions to experiencing the Spirit in an empowering way. Jesus promised the apostles, "You will receive power when the Holy Spirit comes on you" (Acts 1:8), and it seems that "receiving the Spirit" is an abbreviated form of the concept of receiving the power of the Spirit. However, it is not clear in what sense the disciples "received" the Spirit when Jesus breathed on them after His resurrection and said, "Receive the Holy Spirit" (John 20:22).

Filled with the Spirit

Non-charismatic Christians probably find the expression "filled with the Spirit" less offensive than the other main ways of referring to a full empowerment by the Spirit; yet even with this expression there are serious difficulties.

Some Christians fail to make any distinction between being indwelt by the Spirit and being filled with the Spirit, and thus are offended by the suggestion that not all Christians are Spirit-filled. If all Christians were Spirit-filled there would be no point in descriptions such as "Peter, filled with the Holy Spirit, said to them", or "Stephen, full of the Holy Spirit, looked up" (Acts 4:8; 7:55); and there would have been no need for Saul, after his conversion, to be filled with the Spirit when Ananias laid his hands on him (Acts 9:17). There is a further complication, too. Those who have been baptized or filled with the Spirit do not automatically remain "filled" or "full", and therefore one cannot assert that a Christian is "Spirit-filled" or "full of the Spirit" merely because he had an empowering experience of the Spirit at some point in the past. After the threats of the Jewish authorities, the apostles and other believers needed to be refilled in order to preach the gospel boldly (Acts 4:31).

While some believers are under the misapprehension that all Christians are Spirit-filled, a far greater number tend to be shocked by what they consider arrogance on the part of anyone who claims to have been filled with the Spirit. This serious difficulty arises from the fact that the expression "filled with the Spirit" has different meanings for different groups of Christians. For charismatics, it usually means suddenly empowered with the Spirit for witness and service; for non-charismatics, it usually means gradually sanctified or made holy by the Spirit. A charismatic who speaks of his experience of being filled with the

Spirit is not claiming to be holier than a Christian who has not had such an experience. Although a person is sometimes completely delivered from a particular sin at a particular time, sanctification is in general a gradual process in the life of the believer as the indwelling Holy Spirit produces "the fruit of the Spirit" – "love, joy, peace, patience, kindness, goodness, faithfulness, gentleness and self-control" (Gal. 5:22-23).

Whereas fruit needs time to grow, gifts are simply given. After a filling or empowerment with the Spirit, a Christian finds that suddenly he has more spiritual gifts than before, or an increased ability to use gifts already given. Of course, fruit and gifts cannot be completely separated. They are meant to work together, and if the gifts are exercised without the fruit of the Spirit, they are not a good witness to the holiness of Christ: "If I speak in the tongues of men and of angels, but have not love, I am only a resounding gong or a clanging cymbal" (1 Cor. 13:1). Moreover, being baptized or filled with the Spirit should give a boost to the growth of spiritual fruit in a Christian's life because of his sheer gratitude to the Lord; and Luke may intend to imply that the unity and joyful sharing of possessions among the early believers in Jerusalem were due in part to their being filled with the Spirit (Acts 4:31-37). Sometimes, too, the Spirit suddenly bestows a supernaturally intense joy such as Jesus experienced after the return of the seventy-two, when, "full of joy through the Holy Spirit", He burst forth into praise of His Father (Luke 10:21). Nevertheless, there is not necessarily any direct relationship between being filled with the Spirit, and the level of sanctification or spiritual maturity. In order to be equipped as a prophet, John the Baptist was "filled with the Holy Spirit even from birth" (Luke 1:15); and we know from Paul's letters that the Christians at Corinth, though rich in spiritual gifts, were far from mature in holiness.

The different understandings of the meaning of "filled with the Spirit" arise mainly from Paul's exhortation: "Do not get drunk on wine . . .. Instead, be filled with the Spirit" (Eph. 5:18). In the Greek, "be filled with the Spirit" means literally "be being filled with the Spirit", thereby seemingly showing that being filled with the Spirit is the continuous lifelong process of being made holy. But is Paul referring mainly to sanctification? If he is, then his terminology is clearly different from Luke's in the many references to Spirit-filling in both Luke and Acts. Another and more likely explanation appears when Ephesians 5:18-20, which is one sentence in Greek, is interpreted as a unit, and when it is realized that in Greek, "be being filled" can signify a repeated action instead of a continuous action. As we have seen, even the apostles, whom some thought drunk at Pentecost, needed to be filled with the Spirit again (Acts 4:31). What Paul probably means is: "Do not think you are full now merely because you have had an initial filling, or full empowerment, at some time in the past; but go on having repeated fillings with the Spirit." In the rest of this passage he seems to indicate that employing loosed tongues to speak to one another "with psalms, hymns and spiritual songs", to sing to the Lord, and always to give Him thanks, is not only a result, but also a means, of being repeatedly empowered by the Spirit (Eph. 5:19-20). The more we use God's gifts, the more gifts He is likely to give us; and the more we bless God, the more He will bless us.

Regardless of his precise meaning, Paul's exhortation to "be being filled with the Spirit" is a salutary reminder that an initial filling, no matter how fully it may empower a believer for witness and service, does not do away with the necessity to go on walking in the Spirit and being filled with the Spirit. Christians need to be under the control of the Holy Spirit and empowered by Him at all times.

Have I been baptized (filled) with the Spirit?

When a Christian advances beyond the stage of being strung up on the hurdle of theological debates over terminology, he often comes to a firm conviction of the reality and present availability of immediate, full empowerments with the Holy Spirit for witness and service. Naturally, the question that he then asks himself is: "Have I been baptized (or filled) with the Spirit?"

Usually, the experience itself is overwhelming and the results are evident, so the answer seems clear-cut for many. But regardless of whether there has been an overwhelming experience, those who have suddenly begun to speak in an unknown tongue either at or after conversion, and also those who, after conversion, have suddenly received a greatly increased ability to witness for Christ with boldness and freedom, have almost certainly been baptized with the Spirit.

For others, the answer may not be clear-cut. Some have had the ability to witness boldly for Christ from the time of their conversion, and it may not be clear whether their conversion experience included Spirit-baptism. We must be careful not to be dogmatic about which Christians have been baptized with the Spirit.

Far more important than the sometimes-academic question: "Have I been baptized (or filled) with the Spirit?" is the question: "Am I now full of the Spirit?" Regardless of how overwhelming an original experience of Spirit-baptism may have been, or how evident its results in the past, we are leaky vessels that from time to time need to be refilled for service in the power of the Holy Spirit. Furthermore, Paul's exhortation to "be being filled with the Spirit" seems to indicate also that it may be dangerous to regard oneself as "full", because the Lord wants us always to seek more of His power for His service.

Do you want a baptism (filling) with the Spirit?

Strangely, there are some Christians who, though convinced of the availability of full empowerment with the Spirit for the Lord's service, fail to seek it. There are many possible reasons for this.

Some are content to remain at their present level of commitment rather than be given a further privilege that might then place further responsibility upon them. They need to pray for greater zeal for God and greater trust in His love and power. He understands all our circumstances, and sometimes He merely asks people to minister more effectively within their own households.

Some do not realize their importance in the Lord's sight, and thus find it difficult to believe that He would want to fill them (and not only others) with His Spirit and use them in His service. However, the Bible makes it clear that God wants all His people fully equipped for service.

Some are too proud to seek Spirit-baptism for themselves. They find it difficult to come to the point of fully admitting their need to the Lord, to others, or even to themselves. They prefer to go on trying to serve the Lord mainly in their own strength.

One of the most common reasons for failure to seek Spirit-baptism is fear – fear of change, fear of a direct experience of the Spirit, fear of the possibility of speaking in tongues. "But perfect love drives out fear" (1 John 4:18), and as we come to love and trust God more, we can relax in the knowledge that He knows us thoroughly and that His gifts will always be good for us.

Behind everything that holds Christians back from seeking to be filled with the Spirit stands the Evil One. He hates to see people becoming Christians; but if they do become Christians, he then uses every ploy to try to stop them from being fully empowered for Christian witness and service. He wants the Church to be powerless.

Being baptized (filled) with the Holy Spirit

Sometimes the Lord sovereignly baptizes people with the Spirit without their even asking for it, just as He did for Cornelius and his group (Acts 10:44-46). More often, though, some prayer is involved, as in the case of the Samaritans (Acts 8:14-17); and Jesus Himself has promised that our Father in heaven will "give the Holy Spirit to those who ask him" (Luke 11:13).

When a person decides to pray to be filled with the Spirit, he must be sure that he is indeed a child of God through repentance for sin and faith in Christ as Lord and Saviour. He must also be sure of what he is seeking – full empowerment for witness and service. If he is seeking experience for the sake of experience, he will probably be disappointed. If he thinks that the filling with the Spirit for which he is asking is some kind of instant sanctification, then he will certainly be disappointed, and it is doubtful whether he will receive empowerment for service either, since God knows the desires of our hearts and what we mean by our words.

As with all prayers of petition, we should pray with faith and earnestness, desiring to receive all that God has for us, in order to serve Him better. A Christian sometimes finds it helpful to ask someone who has been fully empowered with the Holy Spirit to pray with him as he asks Jesus to fill him, too, with His Spirit.

Laying on of hands, though not essential, may further encourage faith, and is thoroughly Biblical in this situation (see, e.g., Acts 9:17).

One thing is certain: when a person is baptized (or filled) with the Holy Spirit, another dimension of the Christian life is opened up to him, and he is enabled to go forward in greater freedom, exercising more of God's gifts in the service of His Kingdom.

The Gifts of the Spirit

What are spiritual gifts?

Both believers and unbelievers are given natural talents; but in order that the Church might carry out its ministry effectively, God supplies members with spiritual gifts, or special abilities for service. Such gifts differ from natural talents dedicated to God, though they may be exercised through the channel of natural talents, as when evangelism is exercised through singing. In practice it is sometimes difficult to distinguish between the elements of natural talent and spiritual gift in tasks such as Bible teaching and church administration, but where there is only natural talent there is a lack of ability to bring spiritual blessing and growth.

Various spiritual gifts and ministries are listed in Romans 12:6-8, 1 Corinthians 12:8-10 and 28-30, and Ephesians 4:11; and there is no indication that these lists are exhaustive. The gifts of serving or helping, teaching, encouraging, giving, administration or leadership, showing mercy, evangelism, and pastoring do not arouse theological controversy; and most Christians agree that if the gift of apostleship is still available, it is not in its original form or with its original degree of authority. However, there is much controversy about the nature and present availability of the nine gifts listed in 1 Corinthians 12:8-10: word of wisdom, word of knowledge, faith, healing, miracles, prophecy, discerning of spirits, tongues, and interpretation of tongues. Most charismatics believe that this is a list of the more supernatural gifts only, and that all of them are still available today. Some charismatics use the term "spiritual gifts" or "gifts of the Spirit" to refer to these nine gifts alone.

The most obvious feature of the charismatic movement is its refusal to be restricted to only the seemingly more ordinary gifts. Charismatic churches usually claim to be using the whole range of New Testament gifts and ministries, except perhaps apostleship. Indeed, the word "charismatic" is derived from the most frequent New Testament term for spiritual gifts, "charismata". This term implies that they are expressions of divine grace, and thus reminds us that neither the servants nor the ones served deserve these gifts, because they show God's unmerited favour toward us.

The relationship of Spirit-baptism and gifts

When a Christian is baptized (or filled) with the Holy Spirit he is given more "grace", in the sense of God's power for the purpose of ministry; and both Paul and Peter speak of spiritual gifts as the expression of different forms of grace (Rom. 12:6; 1 Peter 4:10). There is, then, an essential link between Spirit-baptism and spiritual gifts. Each filling with the Spirit further empowers for witness and service, thereby resulting ordinarily in an increase in the number of gifts and/or increased effectiveness of gifts already given.

God is sovereign in the distribution of gifts, for the Spirit "gives them to each one, just as he determines" (1 Cor. 12:11). There is no clear Scriptural promise that Spirit-baptism always results in the giving of one or more of the nine gifts listed in 1 Corinthians 12:8-10; but Scripture does clearly indicate that any Christian who has received from the Lord the ability to speak in an unknown tongue has indeed been baptized (or filled) with the Spirit, for it was the evidence of tongues that convinced Peter and other Jewish Christians with him that Cornelius and his group had "received the Holy Spirit" just as they themselves had (Acts 10:44-47; 11:15-17). Although there is no clear Scriptural teaching that only those who have been baptized with the Spirit may receive any of the other eight gifts listed in 1 Corinthians

12:8-10, in practice some, or perhaps all, of these gifts (depending on definitions) are just as rare as tongues in those churches which do not encourage prayer for full empowerment with the Holy Spirit. The fact that only the gifts in this particular list are referred to as "the manifestation of the Spirit" (1 Cor. 12.7) may perhaps imply a special link between Spirit-baptism and these particular gifts.

Some Christians would like to be filled with the Spirit, but fear speaking in tongues. Prior to Pentecost there is no mention of people speaking in other languages when they were filled or empowered with the Spirit, though their tongues were usually loosed in prophecy and praise, as were those of Elizabeth and Zechariah (Luke 1:41-45, 67-79). In Acts, however, tongues are mentioned in three of the five accounts of initial fillings with the Spirit (2:4; 8:17-18; 9:17-18; 10:44-47; and 19:6). Since Pentecost, it seems that one is fairly likely (if one wishes) to have the ability to speak in tongues, at least for private prayer, after being empowered with the Spirit; but it is probable that this gift is often suppressed, sometimes unconsciously, by potential speakers who do not want to receive it. The Holy Spirit does not force people to do anything against their wills, but His gifts are always good for us, and tongues-speaking strengthens the speaker: "He who speaks in a tongue edifies himself" (1 Cor. 14:4). Tongues-speakers claim that even though they do not understand what they are saying, their conviction, commitment, and love are deepened, and their power to minister is increased, by the practice of praying in tongues. No wonder Paul says, "I would like every one of you to speak in tongues", and "I thank God that I speak in tongues more than all of you" (1 Cor. 14:5,18)! When we ask the Lord to fill us with His Spirit, we should desire to receive all that He wants to give us, instead of trying to prevent Him from giving us particular gifts.

There is much controversy about the closeness of the relationship between Spirit-baptism and tongues. Some believe that, since Pentecost, everyone who has been baptized with the Spirit has been given the ability to speak in tongues, and that if he cannot do this, it is only because he is suppressing the gift, consciously or unconsciously. There is no clear Biblical teaching, one way or the other, concerning this theory. Some try to counter it with Paul's question, "Do all speak in tongues?" (1 Cor. 12:30), which implies the answer "No"; but in this context there is no reference to private prayer language for one's own edification. Rather, Paul is reminding the Corinthians that not everyone has a ministry of giving utterances in tongues when the church is assembled. Similarly, "tongues", when listed as one of nine gifts given to different members "for the common good", must refer to public tongues-speaking (1 Cor. 12:7-11).

Though God is sovereign in the distribution of gifts, Paul tells us to seek spiritual gifts, especially those which build up the church: "Eagerly desire spiritual gifts, especially the gift of prophecy"; "He who prophesies is greater than one who speaks in tongues, unless he interprets, so that the church may be edified"; "Try to excel in gifts that build up the church"; "Anyone who speaks in a tongue should pray that he may interpret what he says"; "Be eager to prophesy, and do not forbid speaking in tongues" (1 Cor. 14:1,5,12,13,39). Some Christians deduce from this that it is wrong to seek the gift of tongues; but Paul is merely emphasizing that prophecy and interpretation of tongues are superior to uninterpreted public tongues-speaking. It surely cannot be wrong to seek a private prayer tongue that edifies us, as long as we seek more keenly for gifts that are of greater benefit to others.

Though we should pray for spiritual gifts and be willing to receive whatever God has for us, His glory must always be our chief motivation. We need to seek the Giver more than the gifts and treasure our relationship with Christ above all else.

When are the supernatural gifts to cease?

Before dealing with the question of the cessation of the supernatural gifts, we must consider which spiritual gifts are supernatural. There is a sense in which all the special abilities that God bestows upon Christians for ministry to the Body of Christ are supernatural, since they differ from merely natural talents; but most believers would agree that healing, miracles, discerning of spirits, tongues, and interpretation of tongues are supernatural in a stricter sense.

Not everybody agrees about the nature of the other four gifts listed in 1 Corinthians 12:8-10 – word of wisdom, word of knowledge, faith, and prophecy – but it is a fair assumption that in this context they too refer to the supernatural realm in the stricter sense. All Christians have saving faith, and most also learn to trust the Lord for the more ordinary needs of life; so it is probable that this gift of faith is the special ability to trust God in more spectacular ways, as for healings and miracles – "a faith that can move mountains" (1 Cor. 13:2). The probability that the wisdom, knowledge, and prophecy to which Paul is here referring involve direct revelation imparted by the Holy Spirit is supported by the following references: "What good will I be to you, unless I bring you some revelation or knowledge or prophecy or word of instruction?"; "Everyone has a hymn, or a word of instruction, a revelation, a tongue or an interpretation"; "If a revelation comes to someone who is sitting down, the first speaker should stop" (1 Cor. 14:6,26,30). What we are dealing with, then, is the question of when the nine gifts listed as "the manifestation of the Spirit" are to cease (1 Cor. 12:7).

Paul classifies the supernatural gifts into three categories – faith, speech, and knowledge. He tells the Corinthians he is thankful that "in [Christ] you have been enriched in every way – in all your speaking and in all your knowledge . . .. Therefore you do not lack any spiritual gift" (1 Cor. 1:5-7); and he also exhorts them: "Just as you excel in everything – in faith, in speech, in knowledge . . . – see that you also excel in this grace of giving" (2 Cor. 8:7). Presumably, in the broader sense "faith" includes faith, healing, and miracles; "speech" includes prophecy, tongues, and interpretation of tongues; and "knowledge" includes word of wisdom, word of knowledge, and discerning of spirits.

In 1 Corinthians 13 Paul teaches that prophecy, tongues, and knowledge will all disappear "when perfection comes" (vv.8-10); and there is the clear implication that "a faith that can move mountains" (v.2) will no longer be necessary then, either, any more than voluntary poverty and martyrdom (v.3). It is obvious that "when perfection comes", all nine supernatural gifts will cease. When tongues cease, so must interpretation of tongues; with knowledge would go wisdom and discerning of spirits (and in any case one of the main functions of this last gift will be superfluous when revelatory messages cease); and with extraordinary faith would go healing and miracles. But when will "perfection" come?

Paul says that when "perfection" comes, our knowledge will be complete (vv.9-10), we shall be mature (v.11), "we shall see face to face" instead of a poor reflection, and we shall "know fully", just as we are "fully known" – presumably by the Lord (v.12). By the time we reach verse 12, it has become obvious that Paul is referring to the Lord's return, when perfect knowledge will be given. We still "know in part" and "perfection" has not yet come, so we should expect all the supernatural gifts still to be operating in the Church. Paul's teaching is plain: the supernatural gifts will cease when Christ returns. Only then will they be no longer needed.

That the reference is to Christ's return is confirmed by another passage in this same letter: "Therefore you do not lack any spiritual gift as you eagerly wait for our Lord Jesus Christ to be revealed. He will keep you strong to the end, so that you will be blameless on the day of our Lord Jesus Christ" (1:7-8). With confidence, then, we can declare that all the spiritual gifts may operate, whenever the Lord chooses, right up till Christ returns.

Why do some believe certain gifts have ceased?

Many Christians who assert that the supernatural gifts have ceased base their opinion mainly on 1 Corinthians 13, the very chapter in which Paul teaches that such gifts will cease only when Christ returns! The problem is caused by what the vast majority of Bible scholars now recognize to be misinterpretations of what "perfection" means in Paul's statement that "when perfection comes, the imperfect disappears" (v.10). One misinterpretation is that "perfection" refers to the maturity of the later Church, as contrasted with the immaturity of the early Church which needed "childish ways" such as supernatural gifts; but in the broader context it is clear that Paul uses the illustration, "When I became a man, I put childish ways behind me" (v.11), to mean that, when Christ returns, supernatural gifts will seem childish to us by comparison with the perfect knowledge that will then be given. A closely related misinterpretation is that "perfection" refers to the completion of the canon of New Testament Scripture. The erroneousness of these two views becomes obvious when we consider whether any Christian today would dare to claim that he sees "face to face" and knows "fully, even as [he is] fully known" (v.12).

Other Christians who assert that the supernatural gifts have ceased tend to ignore Paul's teaching to the contrary in 1 Corinthians 13, and base their opinion mainly on the opening of the letter to the Hebrews: "In the past God spoke to our forefathers through the prophets at many times and in various ways, but in these last days he has spoken to us by his Son" (1:1-2). The writer is declaring that before the time of Christ, God often spoke to His people through the various kinds of partial and incomplete revelation given to the Old Testament writers; but that the coming of Christ has inaugurated a new era in which God has spoken to us fully through His own Son, through whom has come the final revelation before His return at the end of the age. The prophecies of the Old Testament are fulfilled in Christ, who is Himself God's full and final revelation.

Even though the writer to the Hebrews says that God has already spoken His last Word for this age, evangelical Christians, whether charismatic or not, are united in their belief that this final revelation is interpreted and expressed in authoritative written form in the New Testament as a whole, including the letter to the Hebrews and other books written after it. The Old Testament was already a completed, authoritative collection by Jesus' time; and as the Holy Spirit continued to work in the hearts of God's people, they came to accept the books of the New Testament as well as the Old as God's Word, to submit to their divine authority, and to collect them together, excluding other writings. The canon of New Testament Scripture was officially fixed in the fourth century, and some Christians find it difficult to understand how anybody could legitimately claim to have any further revelation from the Lord thereafter – more especially since all the New Testament books were written almost certainly by apostles or close associates of apostles. Christ gave the Twelve (with Judas replaced by Matthias), Paul, and perhaps James (the Lord's brother) full authority to act on His behalf, and they became the foundation of the Church in a sense secondary only to that of

Christ Himself. Apostolic authority, which is really Christ's authority, is now exercised through the completed Scriptures. How, then, can the supernatural gifts still function?

However, when we reflect on the implications of the theory that the completion of the canon automatically excludes any further exercise of supernatural gifts, we are led to wonder how these gifts could legitimately have functioned in New Testament times through anybody except Christ and the apostles. If the exercise of these gifts would now be competing with the apostolic authority of the Scriptures, would it not have been competing also with the authority of the apostles during their lifetimes? Yet Paul encourages the proper use of all such gifts as part of the worship of individual congregations.

A related problem posed by the beginning of Hebrews is that it appears to consign to the pre-Christian past, and not merely to the early Church, the "various ways" in which God revealed Himself to and through the "prophets", the Old Testament writers; and these ways included healings, miracles, prophecies, and visions (often a part of the prophetic gift). All of these are found in the New Testament also, both before and after Pentecost, and the recorded examples are not restricted to the ministry of Christ and the apostles. After Pentecost, Philip the Evangelist and Ananias performed healings (Acts 8:7; 9:17-18); Stephen, Philip the Evangelist, and Barnabas performed miracles (Acts 6:8; 8:6,13; 14:3); Agabus, Judas called Barsabbas, Silas, and the four daughters of Philip the Evangelist were all prophets (Acts 11:28; 21:11; 15:22,32; 21:8-9); and Ananias and Cornelius had visions (Acts 9:10-16; 10:3-6). Joel's prophecy quoted by Peter at Pentecost is relevant here:

> In the last days, God says,
> I will pour out my Spirit on all people.
> Your sons and daughters will prophesy,
> your young men will see visions,
> your old men will dream dreams (Acts 2:17).

Since "the last days" will not end until the return of Christ, one would assume from Joel's prophecy that revelatory gifts are available to ordinary Christians now, as they were to those in the early Church; and this assumption agrees with Paul's teaching in

1 Corinthians 12-14. It is clear that some false conclusions have commonly been drawn from the opening words of Hebrews: "In the past God spoke to our forefathers through the prophets at many times and in various ways, but in these last days he has spoken to us by his Son".

The key to reconciling the opening of Hebrews with Joel's prophecy, the teaching of 1 Corinthians 12-14, and the exercise of supernatural gifts in the New Testament Church, is to understand that there are different kinds of revelation with different degrees of authority. The opening of Hebrews is referring to that inspired revelation meant to become part of Scripture. As the very Word of God written, it is infallible, inerrant, and absolutely authoritative for both faith and life. It is redemptive revelation, in that the general theme of every book either deals with or has some relevance to God's grand plan for the redemption of mankind through Christ. In Old Testament times it came through prophets, to whom God gave fragmentary glimpses of His plan by such means as manifestations of Himself, healings, miracles, dreams, visions, prophecies, and interpretations of events. In New Testament times it came through apostles or their close associates, to whom God gave a full view of His plan by means of the Person, life, teachings, death, resurrection, and ascension of His own Son. The apostles had to have seen the risen Christ so that they could bear witness to the resurrection.

On the other hand, Joel's prophecy quoted by Peter, and the teaching of 1 Corinthians 12-14, refer to a different type of revelation altogether; and the exercise of revelatory gifts in the New Testament Church illustrates this difference. Unless spoken by an apostle, prophecies in a known or an unknown language, and words of wisdom and knowledge, were not regarded as infallible, inerrant, or authoritative, for it was understood that they were not the very words of God. They had to be tested in the light of Old Testament Scripture and of apostolic teaching, and the gift of discerning of spirits had to be exercised by the leaders so as to judge whether the utterance was really from the Lord (1 Cor. 12:3; 14:29; 1 John 4:1-3). Such revelation was not redemptive, for instead of giving new insights into God's plan for man's redemption, it encouraged or warned or guided an individual or a group through a prediction such as Agabus's prediction of a famine (Acts 11:28), through an indication of the will of God in a given situation, as when the Holy Spirit indicated that Barnabas and Saul were to be set apart for a special task (Acts 13:1-2), or through a strengthening and comforting message (1 Cor. 14:3), often perhaps in the nature of a timely reminder of God's love and faithfulness even in the midst of a hostile environment.

The canon of Scripture is now closed, but God continues to give the lesser kind of revelation today through the exercise of gifts, just as Paul envisaged; and those churches which are open to such gifts are experiencing great blessing and growth. God reveals nothing new today concerning doctrine or ethics, and messages must be tested in the light of the completed Scriptures and with the aid of the gift of discerning of spirits. The exercise of revelatory gifts does not compete with the authority of the Scriptures, and nor may anything be added to Scripture.

The "faith" gifts are not revelatory in the same sense as the "speech" and "knowledge" gifts are, but they do usually reveal God's power and love. They are not as uncommon today as is sometimes imagined, since in some churches healings are witnessed frequently, and miracles such as the multiplication of food or the raising of somebody from the dead are not unknown. Like the revelatory gifts, "faith" gifts bring great blessing and growth to the churches where they are practised; and in addition, in evangelistic situations they have the special function of "confirming the word" that has been preached so as to help people to believe the gospel. This practice of believing that God will confirm His word by signs is thoroughly Biblical. At Iconium Paul and Barnabas spoke boldly for the Lord, "who confirmed the message of his grace by enabling them to do miraculous signs and wonders" (Acts 14:3); and the writer to the Hebrews asserts that "This salvation, which was first announced by the Lord, was confirmed to us by those who heard him. God also testified to it by signs, wonders and various miracles, and gifts of the Holy Spirit distributed according to his will" (2:3-4).

Those Christians who believe that there can be no genuine gifts of healing and miracles today usually argue that these gifts are no longer needed because the message of salvation through Christ has already been confirmed by the signs performed by

Christ and the apostles. They insist that there is a finality about the statement at the end of Mark: "Then the disciples went out and preached everywhere, and the Lord worked with them and confirmed his word by the signs that accompanied it" (16:20).

There are many problems with this position, quite apart from the textual doubtfulness of Mark 16:9-20. Healing and miracles are often needed to relieve human distress, so they are not performed only for the purpose of confirming the word. Moreover, God confirmed His word by signs precisely so that people would not have to believe only what other people said, and the very nature of such confirmation demands that it be repeatable for each generation and in each new missionary situation. Indeed, in the same section of Mark we are told that the gift of healing is a sign that will accompany those who believe the message preached by the Eleven (16:15-18), and we know from the record in Acts that it certainly was not restricted to these original disciples. Finally, any attempt to restrict the practice of any of the supernatural gifts to apostolic times ignores Paul's teaching in 1 Corinthians 13 that such gifts will cease when Christ returns.

The proper use of spiritual gifts

All spiritual gifts, whether more or less supernatural, are to be used to glorify God and to serve others. We should not neglect our gifts because of false humility or timidity; if the Lord gives someone the gift of evangelism and asks him to share the Good News on a street corner, dare he refuse? On the other hand, we should not display our gifts to glorify ourselves, like a preacher taking pride in his own expressive abilities, or a church member promoting himself through serving. However, it is the more spectacular gifts that seem to lend themselves more readily to the glorification of users who are not sufficiently on guard against the wiles of the Devil. The more spectacular the gift, the more important it is to "test the spirits to see whether they are from God" (1 John 4:1).

When gifts such as prophecy and tongues are used in a congregation today, it is well to observe the rules which Paul laid down to correct abuses in the Corinthian church: "If anyone speaks in a tongue, two – or at the most three – should speak, one at a time, and someone must interpret. . . . Two or three prophets should speak, and the others should weigh carefully what is said" (1 Cor. 14:27,29). However, his ruling that "If there is no interpreter, the speaker should . . . speak to himself and God" (1 Cor. 14:28) shows that an interpretation is not necessary when a tongue is being used in private prayer. Evidently, the speaker's spiritual understanding of what the Holy Spirit is accomplishing through his tongue is sufficient for his prayer of praise or supplication to be acceptable to the Lord.

When God is being truly glorified in the use of a spiritual gift, it follows that others are being truly served. Paul's great chapter on love, 1 Corinthians 13, puts the gifts into perspective and provides a model for exercising them with a great deal of sensitivity to the needs of others. To disregard where others are at in their spiritual walk and use our gifts among them in ways that they do not understand or that make them feel inferior, is unloving, because it is impatient and unkind. In public worship, as many members of the congregation as possible should be encouraged to take a leading role in a part of the service. Only when each member of a church is exercising his gifts, and doing so in accordance with the principle of love, can that church truly be the Body of Christ in its locality and manifest the unity of the Spirit in diversity (1 Cor. 14:26; 12:12-31).

The criterion for the use of spiritual gifts must always be love for God and neighbour. If properly used, they enrich Christians and further God's Kingdom on earth; but if God is not truly glorified and others are not truly served, gifts become stumbling-blocks instead of stepping-stones.

Which Way Ahead?

With regard to charismatic issues, Christians fall into three main groups. There are rapidly growing numbers of charismatic or pentecostal Christians in both pentecostal and more traditional churches; there are those who are totally opposed to everything which the charismatic movement represents, including some who are convinced that it is impossible to be both charismatic and truly evangelical; and there are the majority, who do not feel strongly one way or the other and who are confused and usually quite ignorant about these matters.

In the face of the phenomenal worldwide growth of the charismatic churches, there is an urgent need for every Christian to come to informed decisions about the basic issues: direct experiences of the Holy Spirit, and the supernatural gifts of the Spirit. This booklet has presented strong Biblical evidence to support the conclusion that, either at or after conversion to Christ, people today may directly experience the Spirit and receive His supernatural gifts.

Those Christians who are opposed to the charismatic movement often have a genuine concern about two matters: the peace and unity of their churches, and the sufficiency of Scripture. The preceding chapter has already dealt with the mistaken view that any use of supernatural gifts, and especially "speech" and "knowledge" gifts, threatens the evangelical doctrine of the sufficiency of the completed Scriptures. Revelation from the Lord today does not add to Scripture, since it reveals nothing new about doctrine or ethics. Charismatics have no more of a problem about the sufficiency of Scripture than has any Christian who seeks the advice of a doctor, a lawyer, or a banker with regard to medical, legal, or financial matters; or any Christian who prays for the Lord's guidance about what occupation to choose, or whether to marry a particular Christian person, or which church to join, or where to live and work; or any Christian who feels the need for a personal word of encouragement from another Christian. It is totally unrealistic to "put God in a box" and claim that today He cannot speak to us about anything at all except through Scripture.

With regard to the concern about peace and unity, it is often asserted that charismatic beliefs cause disunity in churches by dividing Christians into inferior and superior. Sadly, some charismatics do tend to feel superior to non-charismatic Christians, just as some non-charismatic Christians tend to feel superior to charismatics and label them as "over-emotional" or "peculiar". However, where there have been any problems, the immediate cause seems to be twofold: some charismatics become so excited about what the Lord is doing in their lives that they unwisely try to push their experience on to others; and these others misinterpret this eagerness and suppose (usually wrongly) that the charismatics are claiming to be superior Christians. Disunity over charismatic beliefs is tragic and unnecessary, but Satan always tries to use every opportunity to stir up trouble among Christians.

Tragic in another way is the fact that great numbers of Christians are missing out on many of God's blessings because of theological prejudice. They welcome the fruit of the Spirit (Gal. 5:22-23) but are closed to several of those gifts of the Spirit that are increasingly evident today. This attitude is surely a form of quenching the Spirit, and must be felt by the Lord as an affront. It is equivalent to trying to control Him, saying, "Thus far, and no further." In the face of growing evidence that in the twentieth and twenty-first centuries the world has seen the mightiest outpouring of the Spirit since Pentecost, one wonders how much longer any Christian will be able to continue to deny the present availability either of direct experiences of the Spirit or of supernatural gifts – unless through an exercise of wilful blindness.

Through Christians who are open to all the dimensions of the Holy Spirit, God is saving many people, healing people's minds and bodies, setting people free from demonic forces, and empowering them fully with the Holy Spirit for witness and service, including joyful worship and the exercise of supernatural gifts. In certain charismatic groups one may also encounter some undesirable excesses, such as disappointment if people do not fall down under God's power in some ministry situations; or blaming people for lack of faith if they are not healed through prayer; or assuming that all illnesses are caused directly by Satanic forces and can all be healed by deliverance or exorcism; or a belief that unless a person can speak in tongues, he has definitely not been fully empowered (baptized or filled) with the Spirit. Nevertheless, a stark contrast exists between a full-blooded Christian faith and a Christian faith that is restricted by traditionalism and fear of change.

The challenge facing Christians today is to try to keep a Biblical balance while at the same time exercising faith to receive all that God has for us. We must live out Paul's instructions: "Do not put out the Spirit's fire; do not treat prophecies with contempt. Test everything. Hold on to the good. Avoid every kind of evil" (1 Thess. 5:19-22). We do need to avoid excesses; but equally, we need to allow the Spirit to illuminate the Word, instead of unwittingly using the Word to oppose the Spirit. We must be both faithful to the Word and open to the Spirit, for only thus can we move into the full flow of God's purposes today as He prepares His Church Universal for Christ's return. We must discover the vital union of Word and Spirit.

About the Author

Alison J. Sherrington has a Master of Arts Degree in English Literature, a Diploma in Ministry, and a Bachelor of Theology Degree. Her first book, published by the University of Queensland Press in 1970, was in the field of literary criticism. *Word and Spirit,* first published in 1991, has been widely read and well received.

After teaching in secondary schools in Australia and Britain and doing editorial work on Bible translations, she held positions in hospital chaplaincy and parish pastoral work. Then followed a long period of caring for her parents at home. She is now devoting most of her time to the founding of Philip House, an inter-denominational women's organization that aims to establish small residential communities of "single" women to proclaim God's word in various ways (www.philiphouse.org).

Alison has been a committed Christian since the age of twelve. Her church background is Presbyterian and Anglican, and she is now worshipping at The Rock Christian Church, Capalaba, in the Brisbane area.

14511687R00023

Made in the USA
Charleston, SC
15 September 2012

simplicity and trust that the Divine Heart of our Omnipotent Father most deeply desires and requests from us without cease, so that He can truly fulfill, both within us and in the world around us, His paternal and parental functions.

How many times do we allow ourselves to be literally led by God the Father, in both the gross and fine details of our daily lives, by following His lead wholeheartedly, despite not knowing ahead of time what is going to happen? How many times do we let ourselves be similarly led by our Father with the fullness of our hearts and minds, even when we suspect that the outcome could be decidedly against our expectations: even in the face of an outcome, or suspected outcome, that would appear to seemingly go against all kinds of reason? Precisely that blinkered reason in fact, for we do not know God's plan, that we so proudly love employing both with ourselves and others, to rationalize and justify the goodness of our decisions and actions.

As human beings living in a post-industrialized world, we have a very distinct, albeit cultivated, impulse to know things ahead of time. When we do not know them, we seek with every ounce of our efforts to know them, to be able to control the outcomes of all events in our lives according to our desires. This impulse is especially prevalent in the Western world, whereby both the intrinsic individual and systemic worldviews are ones predominantly of power and control – both of self and others – to get ahead. But this impulse is directly incompatible with the desires of our Father's Divine Heart, because the said impulse to know, especially to know with certainty, serves nothing but to hinder, partially or completely, our ability to develop and maintain a true relationship of intimacy with our Father, by abandoning ourselves with complete filial trust in His Divine Heart and Hands. We prevent ourselves from participating in the marvel that is the process of mutual, true glorification of God by His children, and of the children of God by the Father Himself, because one of the main keys that unlocks our capacity to enact and fulfill our Father's Divine Will, is to let ourselves rest *passively and fully* in His Heart; so that we can be effectively led by our Father, at every step of the way in our lives.

The Beauty of God the Father

The radiant beauty of God the Father is stunning and the sheer splendor of His Light is immense. When the First Person of the Holy Trinity attracts a soul to Himself, in order to become intimate with her, nothing else matters for that soul. She remains there transfixed, gazing upon our

Father, admiring His infinite beauty and adoring the sweet sound of His Voice. Everything else pales in significance, as the Father fills the soul completely with His Being, causing the soul to profoundly desire never to be separated from Him again. Indeed, she experiences any temporary separations that may occur with a deep and painful ache of longing, because all the soul desires to do is to remain forever in the Father's Embrace.

In such a state of profound intimacy, God the Father and the soul speak, communicating to each other the desires of both their hearts in the simple, but fully love-laden, language that is both the epitome and characteristic of *the* child-Parent relationship. Both our Father and the soul find themselves engaged in profound, mutual enjoyment of each other. In and through His Divine Heart, God the Father caresses, adores, loves, plays with and delights in the ultimate handiwork of His creation: the soul of the human being; at times even making her laugh with His wild, but always harmless, adventurousness. Meanwhile, the soul profoundly explores every aspect of the Father, concurrently adoring and loving Him from the very depths of her being, while being both in and with her real Father.

The soul finds herself experiencing no hesitancy, timidity, or fear, in asking God the Father all kinds of questions, to which latter our Father responds, without fail, with joy and love. He answers even to those questions that we, in our humanity, tend to consider as some of the most unworthy questions that anyone could possibly ask of anyone, let alone of the Almighty Being who is God. The soul finds herself spontaneously doing all the aforementioned while admiring His Essence, consoling the Creator with the entirety of her being – consolation that soothes our Father's wounded Divine Heart and wins multiple graces, by repairing genuinely from the heart, for the indifference shown to Him by the world. Such is a picture of the kind of intimacy that our Father deeply desires to develop and have with each one of us: a relationship freely available to all those who willingly and wholeheartedly enter to live in His Divine Heart.

The Beauty of His Infinite Love – 1

Firm and tender, irreplaceably sweet and gently caressing, is the beauty of Infinite Love; wrapping up, solidly, in His undying Embrace, all those who desire and seek Him with heartfelt genuineness. Never since the Old Testament era has Infinite Love made Himself so felt and available to everyone, in His First Person, flinging wide open those doors of that immense storehouse of His, in which are found His ineffable graces.

Come and take your fill, therefore, says our Father. Come and adorn your soul with beauty, goodness, beneficence and endless providence, within the mighty Arms of Infinite Love Himself. Do not delay to come and embellish your soul, for there will come a time when He will turn His Face away from us and His storehouse will be closed, as part of His Divine Justice. At that time, all those who request to receive graces from our Father will sadly be left unanswered, because we will have squandered that time allotted to us, the present time, in order for us to 'get it together.' Hesitate no more, therefore, in returning to our Father's Heart, that is overflowing with infinite love, so that the most vital parts of our beings – our souls – can be fully endowed with our Father's heavenly treasures.

The Beauty of His Infinite Love – 2

Stepping into the Divine Will of God the Father by deliberately acceding to enter into the boundless confines of His Heart, we enter to live in the Essence who is the ocean of Infinite Love. We become fully immersed in Love Himself: clothed with Him from head to toe, with love both penetrating and oozing from every fiber of our being, serving as a multicolored lens through which we come to perceive every happening, both past and present, in our lives.

When the effulgent Light, both of and who Is our Almighty Father, opens up and enters to reside in the heart of our souls, the ineffable peace, joy and happiness of Heaven penetrate solidly into the core of our beings, causing us to experience impenetrable calmness, lucidity and peace, even in the face of some of the most distressing of human experiences. We become literally rooted in our Father as He so ardently desires. We come to love, despite our stubborn resistance to Love, through fusion with our Father, from the heart of our souls to the Core of His Divine Heart, in, with and through an immeasurably intense flame of Light and Love: Life upon which the entire universe subsists.

It is through the aforementioned process that we can genuinely state that we are not solely living for or with God, but living in and through God, for unless Love Himself graciously deigns to descend into us first, warming us up from our deathly coldness, as mere human beings we are incapable of giving even a modicum of love back to anyone, let alone to our Heavenly Father. Only in and through Love, can we truly come to know the inherent Truth who constitutes love; truth that makes us genuinely capable of selflessly and wholeheartedly loving our enemies more than our own selves. This is the real meaning of living and being in Infinite Love.

The Sweetness of God the Father

Many in our post-Christian day and age think that God the Father is a myth who belongs solely in, and should be confined to, the historical books of Scripture, given that they widely regard these books as socio-cultural constructions of meaning, rather than the immutable, universal Truth. Others believe that our Father is virtually inaccessible, having spoken through the prophets and His Son, Jesus Christ, in all the centuries that have gone by, whereas different others fear our Father as the vengeful and irate God that seems to predominate in the Old Testament – that God often portrayed as tending toward annihilating all and sundry, whenever His Wrath is aroused by the prideful lack of repentance of His people. Meanwhile, others regard our Father as that 'white-bearded ancient guy' who seems to be widely, albeit erroneously, represented in the paintings of so many artists.

Our Father is none of the above. God the Father is very much alive and active, the Almighty of Heaven and earth, whose Being is timeless and ageless, looking no different than His Son. Our Father is, in fact, beautiful Splendor, with His beauty being infinitely breathtaking, while being both vigorous and sweet. In fact, it can be safely said that sweetness is the second most defining, felt characteristic of God the Father – the first is Love – within the context of the development of His intimate relationships with His adoptive children. Our Father has, literally, not stopped speaking to His children, both directly and indirectly, because the greatest delight of His Divine Heart is in being truly intimate with His children as Father. He is firm, as the real Father should be, but immensely sweet, tender and incredibly generous, to the extent that when we give Him something – no matter how small this may be, as long as it is from our hearts – He will never be outdone in generosity. He proceeds to shower us with gifts of grace and other things that we cannot even begin to fathom, in recompense for just having given Him a little of our puny love.

The Cradle of Infinite Love and Joy

Living ongoingly in the Divine Heart of God the Father, is to live in an immeasurably sweet and tender cradle of Infinite Love, while still living on earth: an indissoluble union of adoration, love, joy and bliss, in the midst of the suffering of our earthly toil. In our Father's Heart we find sorely-needed respite and refreshment from life, drinking in the restoration of Life within us, from the Core of His Divine Heart, through the Sacred Heart of Jesus. We experience God the Father holding us in the heart of our souls: consoling us, loving us and helping us, fulfilling the deepest needs of our beings; giving us true hope, peace, love, joy and happiness when we most need them. But for us to receive and experience the fullness of these heavenly gifts, we cannot simply remain distant and gripe, as most of us like to do. We need to both humbly turn to Him and call upon Him as Father, thus touching His Divine Heart with our childlike trust. This causes our Father to be unable to resist our pleas, rapidly descending, in turn, to our sides from His Heavenly Kingdom, in order to completely fulfill His function as Parent.

Living in and with God the Father is quite simple to achieve, given that He profoundly desires to unite all of us, His children, to Himself, encompassing all our hearts in His bosom. We only need to decide to accept Him fully, with true genuineness in our hearts, for our Father to descent spiritually to us, in all the splendor and majesty of His Glory. For when we converse intimately with our Father, simply and openly in a childlike manner, God the Father responds by instantly enveloping us in that delightful cocoon of His love, providing us with everything we may need.

In these our 21st century days, many of us like to think of ourselves as independent, strong and assertive human beings – can do, therefore will do. But in thinking of ourselves in this manner, striving to be so in most, if not every, aspect of our lives, we forget that we cannot be independent of and from God, especially if we really desire to be successful in our lives. For such attempted independence only serves to distance us seriously from our Father, given that we can, in reality, never be truly independent of Him, since He is Life, hence the very underpinning of the structure of life.

Let us, therefore, not allow our vainglorious 'strength' make us willfully lose out on all the help and love we can receive from our beloved Father, even when carrying out the most inimical details of our daily tasks. Let us consent to allow the Most High to carry out His Fatherly function in us, without any impediments from ourselves, so that He can truly infiltrate and participate to the full, in all the intricacies of our lives.

The Softness of God the Father

God the Father is the Alpha and the Omega, yet His softness is remarkable and His tenderness unmistakable, in His daily, intimate dealings with His adoptive children. Gently caressing, infinitely loving and firmly reassuring are His responses, every time that we turn to Him with genuineness of heart and mind. Our Father listens patiently to our endless questions and ramblings, answering them all in and through His perfect Fatherhood, albeit in different ways and at unexpected times. In fact, the manner and time in which our most beloved Father responds to us, can be safely said to never fail to amaze. The firm timbre of His Voice soothingly envelops and gathers the core of our beings, into the profound recesses of His Divine Heart; relieving us of all our worries and lovingly refreshing us by kissing our souls, before letting us fly out again into the midst of our daily duties.

Such is the softness, tenderness and gentleness that we can expect to experience, in our relationship with our Heavenly Father, when we decide to set aside our fears and hesitancies, in order to approach Him and become truly intimate with Him – an intimacy that becomes more deeply experienced, the more we approach Him with simplicity, rather than through the endlessly formal, highly convoluted discourse that so many like using, when talking to or about God. The latter kind of discourse, in fact, serves nothing other than to inflate intellectual and personal egos, while increasing the distance between our Father and ourselves. Hence, the child-Parent relationship that our Father wants so urgently to institute with each us is, in fact, a relationship of profound two-way knowing, loving and living, that can never be either provided or paralleled by anyone else on earth. Such is one of the graces that our Father has reserved for these end times, as part of the fullness of graces. It is freely available to all those who genuinely desire to become true (active-in-relationship) children of God, rather than who choose to simply remain passive members of the People of God.

The Father's Love, Order and Peace

The immeasurable tenderness, sweetness, goodness and firmness of God the Father's love gently, profoundly and most intimately caresses, soothes and excites, with intoxicating joy, all the dimensions of the soul. It is as though our Father is presenting the latter with a large bouquet of infinitely varied and beautiful spiritual kisses and flowers. Through His infinite love for us, the gift to all humanity of His Divine Heart, God the Father both woos and holds the soul, lightly and securely, in a perpetual cocoon of bliss and Peace. This, in turn, sets the soul wildly aflame with Joy, Happiness and reciprocal love for her Father and Creator.

Meanwhile, the Peace of God the Father is a profound interior peace that results in daily and other life occurrences completely losing their power to disturb us, regardless of their nature. In fact, had the greatest disaster happen to occur at such a moment, our Father's Peace would remain both fully present and steadfast within us, in the heart of our souls, serving as the rock upon which we securely maintain our personal 'houses.' This happens because our Father is the Order of creation and where He is welcome and present, neither disorder nor conflict can exist, despite our ongoing, but ultimately futile, attempts to overturn the Divine Order, by perverting the natural order through our seeking to increase chaos and destruction in the world, under the names of knowledge and progress.

If every one of us, therefore, had to set aside daily whatever we are doing for a small period of time, together with all our preconceived notions about the underlying nature of love, order and peace, we would start experiencing the unparalleled transformation of ourselves into our Father's Love, Order and Peace. Hence, discovering and attaining true understanding of the degree to which the order and peace that we know are nothing but man-made shams, in a world seriously ill and becoming undeniably sicker in the most rapid fashion, through all kinds of negativity, destruction, chaos and meaninglessness. We would come to understand by what ruthlessness and to what degree Satan, his angelic minions and earthly agents intend to decimate the people.

After having tasted our Father Himself as Order and Peace, we will discover that we will not want to depart from the confines of His Divine Heart. We will find ourselves, automatically and firmly, setting behind us the intense disorder and conflict of this world, because it will become inacceptable to us any further. This is the manner through which the innermost, hidden needs and desires of our souls will start being met, and the Kingdom of our Father will grow on earth, finally ushering in His Reign in full.

The Tenderness and Mercy of God the Father in the Life Review

The immense tenderness that exudes from our Father's Divine Heart has to be experienced to be truly known. God the Father is the most tender and intensely loving Parent: never pushing any of us beyond what we can endure in the moment, although He continually sets progressively higher targets for us to achieve, to facilitate our spiritual growth in our journey toward holiness. Even when our Father causes us to see, from within His very own Divine Light (Lossky, 1997; the light of Truth), all the sins we have committed in our lifetime and never genuinely repented from, God the Father still remains and acts as the gentlest Father, insofar as we truly acknowledge His Omnipotence and abandon ourselves completely in His Hands, with filial trust. The purifying process referred to herewith is the Life Review, a process that *will* be undergone without fail in our present time, by every human being on earth (Petrisko, 2002). In fact, throughout the entire process of reviewing our sinfulness with us, our Father unfailingly provides us with all the love and mercy that we need from Him, to be able to endure such a process without harm. He gives us mercy that is, in essence and fact, much sweeter, gentler and even more tender than His infinite love. Our Father's mercy is so qualitatively beautiful that some may think that it is better to keep on sinning, in order to obtain more of such mercy from God the Father. However, this is not the way things work, given that two of the things that our Father most abhors are attempted deceit and manipulation of Him.

When the soul both sees and fully understands the pain that she has inflicted, without second thought, upon the ever-loving Father through her sinfulness, especially systematic sinfulness, the soul does not want to do anything but flee rapidly from the Father's Presence. The tangible darkness that exists in the soul, prior to repenting and being forgiven by Jesus Christ as High Priest, make it very hard for the former to tolerate the most pure and intense Light who radiates Himself into every nook and cranny of the soul. But part of our Father's mercy is the fact that He holds the soul even more gently, though steadfastly, in His Divine Embrace, to prevent her from fleeing, while proceeding to cure her from her spiritual sickness through His Son.

Upon experiencing such sweet mercy, the soul then reaches a profound realization of the intrinsic nature of the wounds that she has and deliberately inflicted upon her most beloved Father. The soul also develops a glimmer of understanding of the unmatched love that the One, True and Only Father really has for the soul: a love that our Father does not hesitate to shower upon the soul in the form of ceaseless and surprising graces, after she sincerely repents. Thus, in and through the magnificent power of God the Father's ineffable Mercy, the soul proceeds to nudge closer to her Father rather than flee, concurrently pledging – rather shyly at first – with the profundity of her being, never to wound such tender, Infinite Love again.

To Our Father

The Consecration (Seal) Prayer to God the Father

Heavenly Father, source of Life, Love and Eternal Happiness. You have bestowed upon us the precious gift of life itself. We beg You, Heavenly Father, never allow us to take this gift for granted. What is more, You have called us to holiness. You have called us to participate in Your Divine Family life through, with and in Jesus Christ. We ask that you grant us, in Your Beneficence, all of the graces necessary to live in accord with Your Divine Will and to offer You, at each and every moment, the fullness of our gratitude, our worship, our thanksgiving and our supplication. We formally consecrate ourselves to You, as prodigal children returning to the Father Who loves us. Accept us, put a royal diadem on our finger. Cloak us in royal purple and prepare us for the feast, the banquet, that You have prepared for all Your faithful children. Amen. (Apostolate of the Divine Heart, 2012).

Anyone who says the above prayer with sincerity of heart will receive the Seal of God the Father for their soul (*ibid.*).

The Pater Noster

Our Father, Who art in Heaven, hallowed be Thy Name. Thy Kingdom come. Thy Will be done, on earth as it is in Heaven. Give us this day our daily bread, and forgive us our trespasses as we forgive those who trespass against us. And lead us not into temptation, but deliver us from the Evil One. Deliver us from the person of Satan. Amen.

PART V

THE DIVINE FAMILY

5. THE DIVINE FAMILY

Living In and With the Three Hearts

Only in and through the Three Hearts can we enter into the New Israel – the New Jerusalem (Rv 21:2), because in either neglecting or denying one of the Hearts, we are denying the essential reality of the intricate interplay and interwoven, mystical nature of the Divine Heart of God the Father, the Sacred Heart of Jesus and the Immaculate Heart of Mary. Let us, therefore, deeply ponder on this fact, as it is only through the ladder that constitutes the Three Hearts, through the binding unity of the Holy Spirit, that the heart of our souls can become fused with the Core of our Father's Heart, in order to enter into the New Israel, for when we reject one of the Hearts, we are, in essence, rejecting all of Them. Such is the meaning and process of living in and with that family of ours who is the Divine Family, in the thousand-year Reign of Peace that is soon to ensue.

The Divine Family

Seated on His raised Throne, in all the splendor of His radiant Light and adored, prostrate, by all the heavenly court is God the Father; the Alpha and Omega (Rv 22:13), the Almighty Owner of all creation. Right next to our omnipotent Father is Jesus Christ, the Lamb and the Lion (Rv 5:5-6), standing very tall with a grave look and scepter in His right hand. At Jesus Christ's right hand stands the Virgin Mary, the Woman full of grace (Lk 1:28) and Queen of Heaven and earth (Pius XII, 1954), looking comparatively diminutive in height, in relation to Her Son. Meanwhile, flowing back and forth between all Three is the Holy Spirit, the Breath of Life, Love and Truth between our Family and all mankind (Job 33:4; Jn 14:17). Such is the true picture of our Father's Divine Family (St Andrews Productions, 2009) – how They appear – on the Solemnity of Christ the King. A Family of unsurpassable radiance, majesty and beauty, with love – Infinite and magnificent Love – streaming forth from the Core of the Divine Heart of God the Father, through the Sacred and Immaculate Hearts of Jesus and Mary respectively, floating on the Breath of Holy Spirit, to become fused with the heart of the souls of willing mankind.

The Distribution of Graces by the Divine Family

When graces are given to souls, it is God the Father who grants such graces, with the rest of the Divine Family either agreeing to, or interceding for, the giving of the graces. In essence, our Father gives or consents that the grace requested or required be given by Jesus Christ, through the Holy Spirit, because Jesus is the Administrator of everything that happens in Heaven and on earth. But since the Holy Trinity has willed that nothing reaches mankind unless it first passes through the hands of Mary, the Triune Queen – Daughter of the Father, Mother of the Son and Spouse of the Spirit – and Mother of all mankind, the grace then passes from the hands of Jesus into Mary's hands. Mary, in turn, gives the grace to the Archangels to pass on to the individual's guardian angel, who then passes on the grace to the soul concerned. This is the process of the distribution of graces, from God the Father to mankind, with any and all graces that we receive being a gift of the entire Divine Family.

PART VI

WOUNDING GOD THE FATHER

6. WOUNDING GOD THE FATHER

When We Sin

On the one hand, when we commit venial sin, the presence of both God the Father in the heart of our souls and the Holy Spirit in our souls diminishes, because the Divine Light (Lossky, 1997) cannot neither be experienced nor perceived fully where darkness enters to live. Concurrently, the presence of Jesus Christ becomes very prominent, because at that point we really need His redemptive activity as High Priest, in and through the veil of His ministerial priests, by means of the Sacrament of Reconciliation (CCC, Art. 4). However, after we receive the latter, with sincere purpose of amendment in our hearts and minds, the presence of Jesus diminishes until we receive Him under the veil of the Eucharist, while the presence of both the Father and the Holy Spirit once again shine in their fullness, in our souls.

On the other hand, when we commit mortal sin, we literally end up with complete and total silence from the Triune God (all Persons of the Holy Trinity flee rapidly from us), because we would have deliberately ruptured our relationship with Them, by willfully preferring ourselves, our desires and our wills, over our inheritance. The Divine Light cannot remain where darkness penetrates fully, because we will have foreclosed all possible space. However, even during such events of our handiwork, both our Father and Jesus still do not condemn us: They are too loving and kind to do so. In both essence and fact, we are the ones who end up condemning ourselves, as the Light of inescapable Truth manifests our inner bitter darkness to us, while noting the silence, sadness, grief and sorrow of both God the Father and Jesus at what we have decided to deliberately perpetrate. Furthermore, should any of us happen to die prior to genuinely repenting from such sins, the silence of our Father and Jesus serve as the quiet nod for Satan and his minions to pounce upon us, gleefully claiming our soul eternally for Hell.

In sum, all the sins we commit deeply wound the Divine Heart of God the Father, the Sacred Heart of Jesus, the Holy Spirit and the Heart of the Holy Trinity without fail. This applies even to those venial sins that so many regard as nothing in our post-Christian day and age, because the Triune God is infinite Life, Light and Love, whereas sin is death, darkness and masked (or not-so-masked) hatred. We urgently need to bear in mind that it takes *only one* un-repented and un-confessed mortal sin, in order for us to lose both our souls and our inheritance for eternity.

The Arrow in the Core of the Divine Heart of God the Father

Every time we sin, regardless of the objective gravity of our sins, we plunge an arrow into both the Core of our Father's Divine Heart and the Sacred Heart of Jesus, since both are encompassed in the Divine Heart of God the Father. The more we sin, the thicker the arrow is, that we plunge into our Father's Heart. Meanwhile, the manner in which we sin (e.g., without compunction), the greater is the strength and intensity of the arrow by which we pierce our Father's Divine Heart.

Our sins appear as large, pitch-black stains upon the radiant purity of our Father's Light and Love. However, what wounds God the Father the most is not even that we sin, although every sin that we commit wounds His Heart both at and in its very Core. What pierces our Father the most is the carelessness and coldness – the indifference – with which we sin: as though nothing matters, because sins committed in this manner, irrespective of whether we do so through commission or omission, pierce our Father's Heart the most deeply and painfully, as a very thick arrow enters mercilessly and ruthlessly from one side of the Core of His Divine Heart, to exit right at the other side. In fact, it can be safely stated that if a human being had to undergo such an experience, they would die in an instant, because their heart would literally split up in two.

Our Father knows very well that we will fall into sin, given that we are frail human beings, hence endlessly tempted by our selves, the world and the roaming prince of darkness with his minions. But God the Father is deeply pierced by our ongoing, generalized indifference, in relation to what we do to (1) Him, (2) our souls and (3) our relationship with Him, for all that He desires us to have is Himself as our Father – Infinite Love for eternity. So let us clearly bear in mind our Father's Divine Heart, every time we find ourselves on the verge of sinning, in order not to plunge any more arrows into the Core of His most beautiful Heart. Our Father has suffered enough, from what we have done and keep on doing. It is time, therefore, that we play our parts, since a true child-Father relationship is a two-way street, not a one-way street.

Consoling Our Father

We have both the ability and the power to console our omnipotent and Almighty God – think about that. We, puny little people, essentially incapable of doing anything, including breathing, unless our Divine Father expressly wills or permits it, have been granted the capacity by God the

Father to console Him: man can console his God. Think about that, ponder that, reflect upon that. Precisely due to His omnipotence, many tend to think that God is the One who should be consoling us, rather than the other way around. In fact, this is how most of us act, in our relationship with our Father. We turn to Him, grumpily and half-heartedly, every time we need something; whining and complaining endlessly about our ungratified needs. Then, after He grants our needs and desires, we relegate our Father to the back-burner, ignoring Him completely until our next need arises. If He is sufficiently lucky, we might just give Him some thanks but not more, otherwise we would be 'overdoing it.'

The above is neither fair nor healthy, because the reality is that our Father also needs to be consoled, not just ourselves. God the Father needs our consolation precisely because of our ongoing, heedless wounding of His most Divine Heart, through the ceaseless commission of our sins. The beauty of it all, though, is that we have been granted this ability by God Himself: as mere human creatures, we have been given the power to console the Almighty Father and Creator. Meanwhile, we should bear in mind that the joy of consoling our Heavenly Father can never be matched by anything or anyone else, because nothing greater exists on the face of this earth, other than the ability of mankind to console and love the Father who is God.

Our Father becomes joyous beyond anything that we can possibly imagine, when we console Him from the depth of our hearts: from the heart of our souls. We arouse great and fiery ardor in Him – the burning, white-hot flame of undying Love – when we actively console our Father, because we are, in essence and fact, giving Him back ourselves, as the human beings He had originally intended us to be, as well as our thanksgiving for being able to console Him even by virtue of the fact of being alive.

When we give ourselves to our beloved Father in this way, His joy and delight in us are immense, because we are showing Him that (1) we truly love Him, (2) we really want to be His children eternally, and that (3) He did the right thing in creating us as human beings; despite all the evil we both have committed and continue to commit. We calm our Almighty Father's righteous Wrath, turning away His Justice and softening the latter's blows upon mankind, by alleviating a little of that profound sorrow that our Father feels, in the Core of His Divine Heart. Let us, therefore, not delay any further, in taking care to soothe and console our Father's wounds, in order to truly deserve the title that He has given each and every one of us: that of adoptive children of God.

The Sorrow of Unrequited Love

How often in a single day do we actively or passively fail, to genuinely requite the infinite love of God our Father? How many times do we select, consciously or otherwise, during a day to prefer our own will over His Divine Will? How often do we proceed, without any thought whatsoever, to plunge that unbearably sharp arrow of pain, grief and sorrow into the Core of the Divine Heart of God the Father? And this irrespective of the inherent cruelty and, oftentimes, deliberate insistence on proceeding, despite being aware of the reality of such cruelty?

How many times do we heedlessly or willfully set aside both the Divine mandate and our intrinsic need to love our Father and Maker above all else, in order to prefer something that originates from ourselves? So how can we stand and profess to love our Father, day in and day out – something so many of us encounter little-to-no difficulty in doing – when many of us continue to act as previously described? What are we really waiting for, to put our money where our mouths are: to start opening our hearts and minds, with sincerity and genuineness; rather than with underlying, if not manifest, falsity and hypocrisy, to become able to receive and requite our Father's infinite love?

God the Father has never asked us for much, neither historically nor presently. All that He desires – that He has *ever* desired – is intimacy; true intimacy with His children on earth. All our Father has ever wanted and continues to want is that we accept Him as our One, True and Only Father, while learning to love Him from our hearts with genuineness, childlikeness and simplicity. Have we really become so callous, cynical and stone-hearted, that it is of no import to us whether we respond to our Father's plea or not? The Alpha and Omega of creation, the omnipotent and Almighty God, is acting like a veritable beggar; stooping down to plead with His children on earth to return to Him; to return to live in His divine bosom. So why do we keep on obstinately wounding our beloved Father's Heart, by continuing to refuse to give Him our hearts? God the Father's Name is not solely Infinite Love; it is also Unrequited Love, because of our ongoing hardness of heart and mind, both individually and collectively.

The love exuding from the Core of our Father's Divine Heart is immeasurable. So why do we continue staying away from Him, regardless of the reason for such distance? Our Father's profound desire is to have an intimate relationship of union, through fusion, with each one of us, both in and through the heart of our souls: a relationship the quality of which is unattainable elsewhere. But for God the Father to graciously descend to live in us, with us, for us and through us – to conjoin us to Himself, through His Son and the Holy Spirit – we have to consent to His coming: we have to give ourselves to Him. We have to both *want* and actively *ask* Him to come, otherwise our glorious Father will remain in His heavenly Kingdom, while we remain in this dark world with ever-diminishing assistance, in all dimensions of our present journey on earth. We need to ask our Father to come and He *will* come, but we need to call upon Him with genuine intent in our hearts and minds.

Just think about all this for a moment: God our Almighty and omnipotent Father – the God who certainly needs nothing and no one to Be, since He is complete in His Triune Self – is literally stooping to the level of *asking* us, mere human beings who are capable of doing nothing by ourselves, whether we will accept His Presence in the heart of our souls. What are we waiting for, therefore, to give our Father our *fiat:* at least our individual, if not our collective, "yes?" Such a *fiat* would be heartily proclaimed by all (Zech 14:16) and we would significantly hasten the arrival of our Father and His Kingdom on earth, through the accumulation of our individual fiats, leading up to the collective *fiat.* What more are we desiring, therefore, from our most beloved God, to become once more living arks of the Covenant? Since this would result, in essence and fact, in our entering into the safe haven of the Third Ark.

Our Heavenly Father is calling us to return to live, permanently, in His Divine Heart and this in lofty ways – ways previously considered by many of us as unattainable, since they were hitherto pursued or reserved for those whom we regard as saints. Ways with unmentionable graces being showered upon us, from the Core of His Divine Heart; specifically all those graces that our Father has reserved for these end times. Shall we return to Him, therefore, to live in His divine bosom, or are we going to insist on staying away? What is it going to be? Are we going to give our "yes" to our Eternal Father, or are we going to persist in saying "no?" In which latter case, we would be following our self-will, out of self-love, instead of the Will of Him Who Is and who loves us with Infinite Love?

Do we desire to experience ongoing peace, love, joy and happiness in our lives – literally the Peace, Love, Joy and Happiness of Heaven? For these are the predominant qualities of our true Home, should we desire it to be so, within the deepest recesses of our beings, despite the ongoing denial of so many these days regarding its existence. A home of incomparable beauty, a marvel of its own, achievable even should we be capable of desiring it only on a fractional level, even though such a fraction of desire needs to be present.

Or shall we continue living hand-in-glove with the prince of this world and of the underworld that is Hell, living with and for him who desires nothing but our eternal ruin? Do we want to continue leading an interior and exterior life that, more often than not, leads to hopelessness, misery and despair, in this era of generalized soullessness? For this is a despair and hopelessness that lead solely to misery and eternal darkness, infinitely wounding our Father in the process because He is Hope, Life and Light – and this not even addressing the injury that we inevitably cause our beautiful souls, because souls *are* beautiful; make no mistake about that. Souls are beautiful, glowing orbs when clean, sparkling with crystal clarity in the tender embrace of their Father, Creator and Eternal God. The time is ripe, therefore, for us all to make a choice: a wise choice, an informed choice, as we so proudly like to say – a truly informed choice. So what is this choice of ours going to be?

Whether we choose God the Father or him who likes to work covertly, ever so slyly deceiving many of us into thinking that he does not exist, while being ever so real and alive, we will experience suffering in life, because life is not solely about pleasure and gratification, especially self-gratification; that is merely both individual and collective delusion. But we can choose to make our lives easier or more difficult, depending on the choice that we make. We can choose to go through life as true children of our Father, journeying back Home for Him, with Him, in Him and through Him; greatly alleviated in this journey of ours on earth, by being open to receiving His infinite graces. Graces that *will* be showered upon us abundantly, from that vast storehouse of our Father's – Heaven – when we give Him our unconditional *fiat,* converting our suffering into jewels more precious than any encountered on earth, rather than exponentially potentiating our suffering, by uniting our will with that of the dark one and his minions. Thus what is it going to be? Are we ready to respond appropriately to our Father's call?

Wounding God the Father and Our Souls

Our Father's love for us is infinite and undying, but many of us regularly wound Him and our souls by what we do, think and the manner in which we behave, both toward Him and others. We regularly cause God the Father profound grief, sadness, sorrow and pain, by what we either do or fail to do, on an ongoing basis. Our Father gave Himself for us, in the person of His Son, through the unity of Their Holy Spirit, so that we could be reunited with Him for eternity. But how many of us truly care about the real meaning of all this? How many of us, in essence, give lip-service to all of the above by outwardly professing our Faith, while inwardly, regularly privileging all those desires that stem from ourselves – our egos – instead of from the desires of our Father's Divine Heart? So how can a Father – a *real* Father and our Eternal Father is a true Parent – not be grievously wounded in the Core of His Divine Heart, when as His children we consistently reject and mock the beauty of His love, through our endless rationalizations of why we should not return?

Where is our fidelity? Even our earthly fathers would feel tremendous pain and sorrow at our heartless ways of being and acting, let alone our most tender, sweet and loving Father. For how long, therefore, do we intend to continue in this manner, testing the limits of our Father's patience? How many of us pride ourselves on stating loudly that we believe, for everyone to hear; while, in reality, we are nothing but lukewarm in our relationship with our Father and our God? How can we call ourselves children or People of God, if we keep on stubbornly neglecting our filial-spiritual responsibilities, through a veritable mountain of distancing rationalizations? Let us seriously consider what we are doing, both to ourselves and others, in the course of our daily lives, therefore, to stop wounding the Love of our lives; for when we wound our Father, we are not solely wounding Him. We are also seriously wounding our very own lives, our eternal souls.

The Tears of a Soul

When a soul becomes indissolubly fused with the Core of the Divine Heart of God the Father, through the heart of her soul, she starts experiencing a little of what our Father experiences on a regular basis. She participates in His great Joy, Peace and the indescribable blissfulness of His unparalleled Happiness as the Eternal Light, Love and Life. But she also participates in the sorrows that our Father is made to regularly experience from the deep wounds inflicted upon Him, by the incessantly piercing and ever-increasing coldness, hatred and indifference – the coldness, hatred and indifference of mankind.

The soul cannot help but shed profuse tears whenever our Father is willfully or not-so-willfully ignored, marginalized, ostracized, blasphemed, neglected and abandoned by His children. Especially when such behavior is enacted by those who proudly and loudly state that they believe, while beating their chests. The soul feels the wounds inflicted upon God the Father by her brethren as though they had been directly inflicted upon her: that is, with anguish and the piercing clarity of dagger-like stabs, in the profundity of her heart. It is, in fact, precisely because of the infinity of His Goodness that an arrow pierces our Father's Divine Heart every time we sin, with the arrow becoming thicker, more deeply and intensely plunged into His Heart, according to the deliberateness with which we commit sins.

The soul, then, cannot resist rushing lovingly and tearfully to console our wounded and sorrowful Father, for in consoling Him for the pain that is so callously and unflinchingly inflicted upon Him, the soul feels the palpitations of His Divine Heart being restored to strength, as the pain of His pierced Heart decreases. The soul also hears her Father's sighs: the un-verbalized pleas of profoundly Wounded Love, that in turn console and restore joy to the heart of the soul at being able to repair, in a little way, for the grief and pain endured by our Father. Thus, it is wise to remember that each time we fall into sin, we do not simply wound profoundly the Divine Heart of God the Father. We also pierce the hearts of all those souls who love Him.

To the Stones of the World

Love exists no longer, now, because the world has become extremely cold. And yet, it does not need to be so, were you to return into God the Father's Arms. "Return, return," our Father says; indeed, He will set you free. Yet, you neither return nor listen, because your heart has turned to stone.

What has the world bribed you with, to have made you sell your heart away? Money, power and position? Or the vanity of your 'true' friends? Do you value life so cheaply, that you have thrown yourself away? Or is it that you are 'considering,' ever thinking, but never doing? Do you want Life? "I'll give it to you," our Heavenly Father says. Do you want Love? "I'll give you more than you ever thought." Do you want Freedom? Yes, oh yes, this with certainty you shall indeed have. And finally do you want Liberty? Even this will you will get should you return.

But you sure seem to want none of these, despite espousing that you do, for you cannot even face yourself: you lie, in depth, to your own self. At least be honest, friend; at least be honest with yourself, for engaging in self-deceit is not good for the soul, despite claiming that you do not lie. "I see right through you," our Father says. Yet, you do not see yourself, because your trouble is believing, when believing is indeed seeing. Whatever you want, our Eternal and Almighty Father will give you, insofar as you return. For only in returning, will you ever be able to truly live.

PART VII

THE DIVINE WILL OF GOD THE FATHER

7. THE DIVINE WILL OF GOD THE FATHER

Doing the Divine Will of God the Father

Whenever we unite our wills to our Father's Divine Will, after having decided to return to live in His Divine Heart, God the Father does not hesitate to grant us His covenants of peace and everlasting priesthood, as He had originally granted to the high priest Phinehas in the Old Testament era (Nb 25:10-13; Bartolo-Abela, 2011). We also win, from our Father, the right to expiate acceptably in His sight for others, because we end up developing the same zeal and love for His Commandments and for souls as He does. Thus, we can obtain countless graces from our Heavenly Father in this manner, both for ourselves and others, including the return of lukewarm and/or obstinate souls to our Father and Creator.

We become adoptive children of God the Father in essence, rather than in name only, because fulfilling the desires of His Divine Heart becomes our greatest desire. All this leads us to actively fulfill our roles as "a kingdom of priests to serve his God and Father (Rv 1:6) . . . a line of kings and priests for God" (Rv 5:10): "a holy race, a royal priesthood" (1 P 2:9; Paul VI, 1964) who serve as much-needed instruments of our Father's Peace, Joy, Love and Happiness, in a world almost completely inundated with darkness.

Importance of Fidelity in the Union of Wills

How many of us promise or have promised things to God the Father, then did not keep our word to Him, either partially or fully, hence wounding Him deeply? How many of us have first made promises, only to proceed to unhesitatingly come up with all sorts of nuanced rationalizations, in order to break our promises to Him? Every time we carry out such a process, formulating rationalizations (and endless ones at that) to justify retracting or otherwise violating our promises to God the Father, our actions are tantamount to our giving someone very close and dear to us a most precious gift, then showing up sooner or later saying, "Hey, you know what? I want my gift back because (insert your favorite rationalization here)." In fact, if someone had to behave toward us in this manner, many of us would not think twice to consider such a person quite rude and disrespectful. We would certainly lose the trust that we may have reposed in them. But many, if not most, of us do not hesitate to act precisely in manner with our Father, in relation to all the gifts we 'give' Him through promises we do not keep.

It is important for us, therefore, to recall that gifts – as promises – that we give our Father are never to be recalled, no matter what it may take from us with regard to our keeping such promises and carrying them out. Irrespective of whether we become inconvenienced in our lives, because of the gifts of promises that we may have given our Father, we need to remain faithful to our word, otherwise we will bring down upon us our Father's displeasure. This is what joining our wills to God the Father's Divine Will is about: fidelity – true fidelity – in our highly individualized and commoditized day and age. It is precisely our fidelity to the carrying out of our promises, within the context of ongoing situational difficulties, which mark us out as true children of our Father, for only by fidelity in the union of wills, can we can ever fulfill the greatest commandment of all: the first Commandment (Mt 22:37-38).

The Beauty of Living in the Father's Divine Will

The beauty of living in God the Father's Divine Will is that we experience immeasurable freedom and liberty, from the imprisoning chains of ourselves, when we seriously set aside our wills to do His Will. Such freedom and liberty become the norm, because we take on for ourselves the inestimable freedom of our Father Himself, with nothing greater existing that is so beautiful and liberating in its perfection. Everything that our Father has becomes ours, while everything we have becomes His, in a reciprocal, ever-increasing relationship characterized daily by the most intimate, filial-Parental Love.

However, for all of the above to happen, for us to experience such freedom and liberty, we need to decisively and constantly set aside ourselves and our egos, in order to actively carry out our personal-spiritual contributions to the child-Parent relationship. We cannot simply sit back and expect it to happen on its own, or expect others, including our Father Himself, to do our work for us. First, because that is not the way things work; and second, because we will only be fooling ourselves, since we will not grow in our lives, as spiritual human beings and adoptive children of the Father. In deciding to integrate our Father's Divine Will, therefore, into our often recalcitrant wills, we need to open up space for Him, so that He can operate in us, through us, for us and with us; because, in so doing, His Will starts operating in us and we inevitably start living in the very freedom and liberty of Heaven.

PART VIII

THE DIVINE HEART AND WILL OF GOD THE FATHER: INFINITE LOVE

8. THE DIVINE HEART AND WILL OF GOD THE FATHER: INFINITE LOVE

The Divine Heart and Will of God the Father: Infinite Love

When we return to live in our Father's Divine Heart, we re-enter to live in His Divine Will, because through our act of returning we unite our wills to His. However, when we unite our wills with our Father's Will, in the moment-to-moment living of our daily lives, we find that we are, without fail, living in the cradle of Infinite Love. So when we return to live in our Father's Heart, we are returning to live in, with, for and through Infinite Love, because God the Father's Divine Heart, Will and Infinite Love are all an intricate part of each other.

The Divine Heart and Will of God the Father: Heavenly Peace

Living in the Divine Heart and Will of God the Father means that we enter to live in the peace of Heaven, as our Father is Peace Himself, thus He exudes peace: the peace that the world and all mankind so greatly need, but that they seriously lack. It is from the Core of our Father's Divine Heart that heavenly peace radiates forth, floating marvelously throughout the boundless confines of His Divine Will, interwoven with infinite love. Hence, when we return to live in our Father's Will, through our ongoing *fiat* to His Divine Heart, we enter to live in Peace, as His Heart, Will and Peace are One, in both essence and being. Moreover, it is precisely upon the territory of our souls, specifically in and through the heart of our souls, by means of our "yes," that Heaven and earth become joined, bringing down the peace of Heaven into our severely peace-starved world.

The Interpenetration of Love

When a soul becomes fused with God the Father, in essence becoming and being fully an adoptive child of the Father, an interpenetration of love occurs between both the Father and the soul. Infinite love descends directly from God the Father, into the heart of the soul from the Core of His Divine Heart, inundating the entire being of the soul. Due to the immensity, purity, intensity, warmth and fragrance of the love that our Father showers upon the soul, the latter cannot fail to respond in kind. Without hesitation she turns to the Father in response, just like a flower that has suddenly opened up and bloomed, giving our Father great joy and happiness in return: a return that most deeply touches the Father's Heart, because of the genuineness of love that the soul starts manifesting both for and toward the Father.

From then onward, nothing exists for the soul externally to the desires of God the Father, because His Divine Will automatically becomes part and parcel of the soul's will. Such is the interpenetration of love that occurs, from the Core of the Divine Heart of the Father directly into the heart of the soul, whenever a soul – any little soul – becomes fully united with our Almighty Father. It is an indescribably beautiful closeness, tenderness, gentleness, surety and peace that occur, within the intimate dance of reciprocal love that typifies the sweet, irreplaceable intimacy of the soul with her Eternal Father. The above is an illustration of the actual process of true intimacy, when a child decides to become united with our One and Only real Father; a unity that is, in essence and fact, the commencement of the fullness of our inheritance (Paul VI, 1964).

A Fusion of Hearts

From the Core of the Divine Heart of God the Father radiates forth all Life, Light and Love, because He is the Creator. It is from this very Core, that can be considered as the heart of the Divine Heart, that our Father is united in Oneness with the Sacred Heart of Jesus Christ, because all of the aforementioned originates from the fusion of these two Hearts (Jn 14:10-11), through the binding unity of the Father's Breath Who is the Holy Spirit (Job 27:3).

Jesus Christ has always been enveloped in the Core of the Father's Divine Heart, since prior to the beginning of time (Jn 1:1-3). In fact, everything that comes to us from God the Father, in terms of graces and other gifts, originates in the Core of our Father's Heart and passes through the Sacred Heart of Jesus, in and through the Holy Spirit. But how does all this relate to our needs while here on earth, especially with regard to the progress in holiness of our souls? Specifically, how does the fusion of the Divine and Sacred Hearts relate to our ability to unify our souls, with those of our Father, our Brother and the Immaculate Heart of Mary our Mother?

Being full of grace as the predestined Daughter of the Father, Mother of the Son and Spouse of the Spirit, the Immaculate Heart of Mary is fused both singularly with the heart of the Father's Divine Heart, the Sacred Heart of Jesus and the Holy Spirit, as well as multiply with and through the Heart of the Holy Trinity; with all intimate communication between the Divine Family occurring in and through their fused Hearts. How is this relevant, though, to the process that the soul spiritually undergoes while still living on earth, upon becoming united with the entire Divine Family?

When a soul becomes united with the Divine Heart of God the Father, in essence she becomes fused, from the heart of the Divine Heart directly to the heart of her soul – a most intimate part of the human soul that only the Father as Creator can access and into which He inevitably descends as dazzling Life, Light and Love. But given that the heart of our Father's Divine Heart is fused both with the Sacred Heart of Jesus and the Immaculate Heart of Mary, the soul who becomes fused with the Father automatically becomes similarly united with the Hearts of Jesus and Mary, for everything passes through and is consented to by their Hearts, prior to reaching the individual soul. This process occurs because Their Hearts and Wills are in perfect, mirroring union with the Divine Heart and Will of God the Father. Additionally, every time the soul receives the Body and Blood of Christ in the Eucharist, she is receiving the Heart of God Himself in both essence and metaphysical being.

Communication, therefore, between the Divine Family (the Triune God and the Triune Queen) with the soul occurs in, from, with and through the Three Hearts, in the very heart of God the Father's Divine Heart; flowing most intimately and directly into the heart of the soul, of the human being. Such is both the actual process and meaning whereby the Divine Heart of God the Father Encompasses All Hearts with Infinite Love. It is the process of joining together of Heaven and earth, the beginning of the New Israel that we have been ongoingly asking our Father for, through the Lord's Prayer: "Thy Kingdom come" (Mt 6:10).

The Freedom of Living in Infinite Love

Living in the infinite love of God the Father's Divine Heart, we experience a freedom, a liberation, of both soul and spirit previously unknown. All the shackles of our past are broken and the impossible becomes possible, whereas the dullest of tasks becomes joyous. Peace, Joy, Love and Happiness inundate our whole being, regardless of what we may be doing, leading us to live our daily lives joined to Heaven while still living on earth.

Being joined with Heaven, however, does not adequately describe the felt experience of what actually happens to us, when we enter to live in the Divine Heart of God our Father. For the Spirit of our Father, Who emerges from the Core of the Father's Heart, literally joins our souls to Himself, leading both our Father and ourselves to live not solely with each other, but *in* each other, at every moment of our lives. We become small containers of goodness that suddenly find themselves completely immersed in and filled with the infinite ocean of Goodness, Sweetness, Love and Peace; a verbally inexpressible infinity of Love, Beneficence, Tenderness, Joy and Happiness that cannot be found elsewhere.

This is the real meaning of the beginning of the coming of our Father's Kingdom on earth, the New Israel, when by our *fiat* we consent that God the Father infuses these qualities of Heaven into our souls, making such qualities the very essence of the heart of our souls. The Goodness, Sweetness, Love, Peace, Beneficence, Tenderness, Joy and Happiness of the Father ceaselessly overflow and radiate onto everything we do henceforth, making us small, but ever-growing, beacons of light amidst the pathways of this darkness-saturated world.

We enter into a harmonious rhythm of back-and-forth dance, fully in keeping with and confirming of the natural order, whereby both our Father and ourselves take immeasurable delight in reciprocally glorifying each other. We utter extremely joyous and most intimate, profound calls of adoration and love to our infinitely loving and tender Father who is our God – the epitome of heart-to-Heart communication – both the origin and spurring of the said calls within ourselves come directly from and through the Holy Spirit. Working and living in this manner, therefore, we not only spiritualize, but actively divinize, everything we do in our daily lives, because it is not solely ourselves who are acting in the moment but God the Father Himself is acting in us, with us, through us and for us, as we live in Him, with Him, through Him and for Him. Such is the process through which we glorify our Father in His Essence and Presence, in and through that epitome of relationships that is the child-Father relationship.

The Simplicity of Knowing Infinite Love

To know and live in God the Father is extremely simple: all we need to do is to decide, sincerely and genuinely, to return and give ourselves to Him; then we start truly knowing Him and living in Him, enjoying at every instance of our earthly lives the joy, love, peace and happiness of

Heaven. But how do we achieve this, when we have been away from our Father's House, many of us for a very long time?

First, our Almighty Father loves us with a love that is infinite: a love both originating in and flowing incessantly from the Core of His Divine Heart, like a never-ending stream of Life – both a Parental and Paternal love that are frantically calling us to return, despite our ever-growing stubbornness and willfulness, in order to keep us safe and sound in every aspect of our beings. We may try to envision such love or attempt to understand it with the intellectual nature of our minds, but we will never be able to truly comprehend it - especially its Infinity and Intensity – unless we open ourselves up to our Father. We need to open up our hearts to our Heavenly Father, in order to experience Him within ourselves, to become able to truly start understanding the immensity and incomparability of what this is all about.

Second, we need to accept to do our part to return to Him, because God the Father will *never* override our free will, no matter how much we pain Him, with so many of our choices – choices that do nothing but severely cloud the clarity, purity and integrity of our eternal souls. We need to (1) consent to return to Our Father, (2) get ourselves cleaned up in our hearts and souls from all the grime that presently exists therein; (3) accept that He *will* come to us, and (4) call Him to ourselves by giving ourselves unconditionally to Him. When we do this God our Almighty Father rapidly descends to live *in* us and *with* us, as He has always desired to do from the beginning of time (Gn. 1 & 2). However, when we do not give ourselves in this manner, our Father keeps on awaiting us on the sidelines, like a sorrowing but ever-respectful Parent: He begs us to accept and let Him in, but does not force our free-will boundaries.

Meanwhile, after having carried out all of the aforementioned four steps, getting to know and live in and with God the Father becomes 'a piece of cake,' because of the inordinate amount of graces that He consequently showers down upon us. We start continually feeling His Presence all around us, both inside and outside of us; we start perceiving His Presence everywhere and become truly capable of developing and maintaining a real relationship of desired intimacy with Him – that special and highly-desired intimacy between Father and privileged child, whereby both communicate with each other in the infinite confines of His Divine Love, Heart and Will. In sum, the doors of God the Father's 'storehouse' are presently, mercifully wide open for each one of us His children, to return to live within His Divine Heart. Come, come and take your fill, therefore, of all the freely- and easily-available graces and love, before the storehouse doors are closed and Heaven stops responding in Justice.

More on God the Father – 1

Sitting atop of all creation, in His Heavenly Kingdom, is our Father, holding us securely in His Divine Heart, nested in His Core of Light and Life, to keep us safely ensconced in His infinite love. Safe from the despicable schemes and endless ravages of the enemy, upon every aspect of our lives and selves; that enemy, the Red Dragon (Rv 12:3) who, with his sycophant minions including the first and second beasts (Rv 13:1, 13:11), do not rest in their ever-increasing and furious attempts, to claim our eternal souls for themselves. Until they are bound anew, in the abyss of Hell by Michael, the prince of the Heavenly court; conjoined with those supplications of ours that arise to Heaven, in and through the binding chain of Mary's Rosary (Rv 20:1-3) and the Precious Blood of Jesus Christ.

Our Father places situations and people in our midst, to both challenge us to grow increasingly toward Him and fulfill the deepest and most craven needs of our souls, acting intermittently on our behalf, even if we simply utter a pitiful and incomplete plea to Him, from the depths of our hearts. Our Heavenly Father gives us gifts, sweetly and playfully presenting them to us in some of the most surprising, but endlessly delightful, ways; warming up our hearts, minds and souls with joy and happiness, while providing us with everything we need, throughout our daily lives on earth, as He did with the Israelites of old. He makes it so that we do not have to worry, or suffer anxiety and fear, over our futures, if we abandon ourselves with complete filial trust in His Mighty Hands and Divine Providence.

How many of us, therefore, can honestly say that we have ever allowed ourselves to truly wallow in such perfect Paternal and Parental Love, in our lives? How many of us have profoundly desired to be the recipients of such fatherly love, yet have repeatedly come away disappointed to say the least, given the behaviors of some earthly fathers? And yet, this is the true Face of God the Father; He is both freely and readily available, to any and all who truly desire to welcome Him into their hearts as Father. Our Father is right on the doorstep of our hearts, pleading with us and begging us, incessantly, to let Him into ourselves and our lives, so that He can really be our Father in every sense of the word. Such is the incomparable and momentous desire of our holy and omnipotent Father.

God the Father has decided that it is high time that He re-enters into the lives of His children on earth, and this in a much more direct way than what most of us have become used to: namely, in and through the child-Parent relationship that had existed prior to Adam's Fall. It is comparable, but not analogous, to the way the Father's Presence had been present among men during the Old Testament era, whereby He had lived among His children, the Israelites, in the physical Ark of the Covenant. The way, therefore, that is slowly but surely ripping away that punitive veil of time and space existent between Heaven and earth, to finally herald in the Reign of God the Father on earth: the Glorious (Eucharistic) Reign in the era of the Holy Spirit, in and through the Divine Will.

More on God the Father – 2

God the Father paternally consoles us when we are sad, He gives us His Peace when we are fearful, He restores hope and Light in our souls when everything around us is relentlessly falling to pieces and we are about to despair. He opens doors for us that we would never consider, let alone open, by ourselves. He gives us His infinite love when we do not deserve an ounce of it and keeps on repeatedly forgiving us, no matter how much we keep on wounding Him, as long as we repent sincerely. Our Father actively participates in our lives, literally divinizing them, when we allow Him to enter into every aspect of our earthly lives, by opening our hearts to Him. He provides us with warmth and shelter, even when we have generally not earned it. He puts food on our tables, even though we seem to ruthlessly enjoy destroying everything He creates, He clothes and protects us in every way, keeping us safe and healthy, even though we are severely wasteful and rebellious. God the Father brings us gently back into His Divine Heart every time we stray into dangerous territory, ensuring that we are not lost, both in the present and in eternity. That is a true picture of who our Father is throughout our daily lives: the Eternal God of Providence, Mercy and Love that is true Life.

PART IX

GOD THE FATHER AND JESUS CHRIST

9. GOD THE FATHER AND JESUS CHRIST

The Father on the Cross with His Son: Infinite Love

God the Father was both in His Kingdom and present on the Cross over two thousand years ago, when Jesus Christ was crucified on Mount Golgotha, despite our ongoing disregard for and denial of this reality: our Father was on the Cross in Spirit. As the Father who is Infinite Love, the Almighty Father experienced inexpressible anguish, grief, sorrow and pain in the Core of His Divine Heart, for everything that Jesus Christ had to suffer in order to redeem us, so that the gate to Him Who Is Heaven would be re-opened, making it possible for us to be everlastingly reunited with our Father. Specifically, God the Father experienced the unspeakable anguish, grief, pain and sorrow of *the* Perfect Father, over *the* indescribable suffering of *the* Perfect Son; and this is just the tip of the iceberg of what the Father had to endure on that Redemptive day for what we have done, do and continue unhesitatingly to do.

For God the Father also experienced great anguish, grief, pain and sorrow over the martyrdom of His most beloved Daughter Mary, a martyrdom that has remained largely hidden to this day. This together with the additional grief and anguish that our Father had to endure, through knowing exactly how many souls would still insist on being lost eternally through their willful choices, both on and after that day, until the end of the world. All the aforementioned was exponentially compounded by the need for our Father to necessarily proceed with the Everlasting Sacrifice, in order for us undeserving creatures to be able to reconcile ourselves fully with Him.

Even in the present, God the First Person suffer greatly, with the Heart of the perfect Father, over having to punish any of His adoptive children. However, because He is also Order and Righteousness, His similarly perfect Justice cannot but demand appropriate reparation, otherwise He would not be the perfect Being. Thus, our Almighty Father had to allow His Wrath to emerge despite His own suffering on that day, in order for Justice to be everlastingly satisfied. It was a Wrath that was still Mercy in itself, because God the Father literally crucified part of Himself, in and through His Spirit, in the Person of His Son, in reparation for our misdeeds instead of crucifying us, as we so richly deserve. Consequently, it is imperative for us to be aware of the true extent of our Father's love for us, if we really want to both be and be known as adoptive children of the Father. Failing to do so, we will be nothing but ungrateful creatures.

The Mystical Body of the Father

As the Church is the Mystical Body of Jesus Christ, so is She similarly the Mystical Body of the Father, because God the Father and Jesus Christ are One in Spirit, through the Holy Spirit, albeit different in Person. Meanwhile, as Jesus Christ went through His Passion and Crucifixion, in order to both redeem us and establish His Church on earth, so will the Mystical Body of the Father and the Son similarly go through everything that Christ went through, in order for the Reign of God the Father to ensue fully on earth in all its glory (Rv 20:1-6).

PART X

THE REIGN OF GOD THE FATHER

10. THE REIGN OF GOD THE FATHER

The Current State of the World

Love for God, especially God the Father, our Creator, has become largely absent in the hearts, minds and souls of mankind. Such an absence has, naturally, caused the world to become spiritually barren – a veritable desert, a wilderness – once again, because hope, love and charity have died in the hearts of most individuals. Yet, despite this dire and seemingly ever-worsening situation, we tend to experience ongoing and considerable difficulty in both perceiving and acknowledging this reality even to ourselves. This is happening because many, if not most, of us have either not or never allowed ourselves to be really wooed and taken over by the ultimate force of True Love; so we have struggled and continue struggling to understand what love really is: our Father's Infinite Love.

In our discourses, policies, politics and practices, as well as during the course of our daily lives, we find ourselves talking about love, when in reality we do not know Love. We talk righteously about freedom, when we have little to no idea what real Freedom is; and we pontificate ceaselessly about liberty, when we have no clue about the inherent nature of true Liberty. We talk ever so loudly and proudly about god, both in our lives and on the media, when so many of us have never taken either the time or the interest to attempt to develop and maintain an intimate relationship with the Triune God, but most especially our Almighty Father. Many, if not most, in fact have never developed that kind of relationship without which none of us can ever truly come to know God, in terms of the little that any of us can ever possibly know of Him and in Him, precisely because of His Infinity and Omnipotence.

All of the above is occurring because we proudly do not want to worship. We do not want to bow our heads, we do not want to open up and soften our hearts and minds, and we most certainly have no desire to humble ourselves, by bending our knees in front of our Maker and Father. We both want and expect God to accommodate us, in the vast majority, if not all, of our entitled ways, rather than the other way round. Deep down in our hearts, therefore, we find ourselves having little to no desire to change our ways, infinitely preferring that our Father change His ways instead, to suit our proud selves. Moreover, all of this is happening despite the fact that many of us do seek and desire, both consciously and unconsciously, to find and have God in our lives. However, we only want a god who will fit in nicely and neatly with our man-made notions of who and what God should be like: a god who will not inconveniently and, at times, uncomfortably upset the apple-carts of our present lives and lifestyles.

We conveniently choose to set aside and forget the fact that some, if not most, of our present lifestyles go directly against God, wounding His Divine Heart and Will, by violating His divine Law. However, instead of dispensing with our false notions that we like to consider as our right to freedom, we deliberately select, through ceaseless rationalizations, to make away with the only Father who has truly loved and continues to infinitely love us in our entireties, despite all our obstinacy and willful rebellion. In fact, we proceed to unhesitatingly erect several false gods under various names, which gods are no different in kind than the entirety of the Ba'als present and worshiped during ancient times. Consequently, our world, both our local and global worlds, have become desolate, neo-pagan deserts, more than two thousand years after the birth of Christianity.

Neglecting God the Father Individually and Institutionally

We have, in both essence and fact, neglected God the Father both individually and institutionally, because when we pray, we pray or are aware of praying to anyone but Him. Many, if not most, of us pray endlessly to the saints, to the Blessed Virgin Mary and to Jesus Christ, but only rarely do we pray directly to our Heavenly Father. Why have we reached this point of neglect and abandonment of God the Father, when anyone whom the Father sent us – including Jesus Christ and Mary – came precisely to show us the way back to our Father? Why have so many of us seem to have lost the most basic understanding of all: that the Holy Sacrifice of the Mass is, in actuality, *the* prayer of Sacrifice, worship and praise to God the Almighty Father?

We have reached this point, both individually and institutionally, because many come to believe in the depths of their hearts that God the Father is either unreachable or absent. We have learned to erroneously perceive our Father as a stern, unapproachable God. Hence, we have let ourselves become conditioned into thinking that it is better for us to go the indirect route in our spiritual lives, very frequently proceeding to carelessly offer up words of prayer and conversation to our Father, with such offerings rarely coming from the depths of our hearts, minds and souls.

We have essentially marginalized the Presence of our beloved, sweet, very tender, gentle and infinitely loving Father, deeply grieving His already-wounded Divine Heart by our ongoing neglect and abandonment of Him. We have made God the Father, the First Person of the Holy Trinity, from Whom everything and everyone else originate, come second if not third, fourth, or fifth – and this is being kind. Is this the manner in which we should treat our most beloved Father without Whom we would not exist, when many of us treat our earthly fathers in better ways? Him Whom we should adore and love, with the entirety of our bodies, minds, hearts and souls?

We need to re-acquire the fundamental realization that without God the Father there would be nothing and no one else. We need to start re-comprehending at a gut level the Truth that without our Heavenly Father, both individually and institutionally, there neither is nor can ever be any fullness of our inheritance (Paul VI, 1964), because it is the Almighty Himself Who Is the Inheritance. Therefore, we need to understand that everything we do, including the end object of all our prayers, is none other than God the Father Himself: the First Person of the Holy Trinity, because He is the Alpha and Omega.

Defending Our Father

How often do we stand up for God the Father, acting like true adoptive children by defending Him both privately and/or publicly to others, when the need arises? Something that is, in essence and fact, very sorely needed in this de-Christianized day and age. How often do we either neglect or outrightly refuse to defend our Father, out of fear of incurring rejection and retaliation from others, or even just the possibility of not being liked as much as before, if we had to take a stand and speak up for our Father?

How many times in the course of our daily lives are we acting as cowards and hypocrites? In essence and fact, as end-times Pharisees, instead of as men and women of fiber, because we are ashamed to own up to Who and What our Father really Is? Hence, preferring to protect our human hides instead, under various beautifully sounding rationalizations? Every time someone insults, denigrates, or attacks a member of our earthly families, we are generally quite prompt in responding, to vigorously defend the said member of our clan. But when it comes time to defend any of the Members of our Divine Family, especially Its Head, we suddenly become severely lacking in both responsiveness and responsibility.

We need to recall that Jesus Christ said that, "Every one therefore that shall confess Me before men, I will also confess him before My Father who is in Heaven. But he that shall deny Me before men, I will also deny him before My Father in Heaven" (Mt 10:32-33). This similarly applies to ourselves, with regard to our ongoing relationship with God the Father, because Jesus Christ came to show us the Way to our Father, making it imperative that we courageously stand up for and with Him before those who covertly or overtly denigrate, disrespect, insult, ridicule and flagrantly attack Him and His Sacred Mysteries. We need to take such a stand regardless of what it may personally cost us in consequence, otherwise apart from grievously wounding our Father most deeply, in His most tender Divine Heart, God the Father will rightfully decline knowing us and knowing us as His children, when the appropriate time arrives.

Returning to the Father

Returning to God the Father means returning to live at Home in His Divine Heart and Will, for the Core of our Father's Heart is the Kingdom of Heaven: Infinite Love. It is the Kingdom which has been promised to us from eternity and to which we are the rightful heirs, should we choose to exercise our right of proceeding to claim our legitimate inheritance (Paul VI, 1964). So when we decide to return Home to our Father, by accepting to return to live in His bosom, we are essentially returning to live in that precise place from where our souls have both originated and which is the Residence of the Father's Thought, Word and Spirit.

The Reign of God the Father in the Eucharistic Era of the Holy Spirit

The forthcoming Glorious (Eucharistic) Reign is the coming fully on earth of the Kingdom of God the Father, that we have been asking for over two thousand years, because it is the coming down from Heaven of the New Israel (the New Jerusalem; Bartolo-Abela, 2011; Is 35:1-10, 51:3-11, 60:1-22, 62:1-12, 65:17-25, 66:10-24; Rv 3:10-12, 14:1, 21:1-4, 21:10-27, 22:1-5) which constitutes the Reign of the Father on earth with the Divine Family, in the Kingdom of His Divine Will (Piccarreta, 1899-1938/2007), in the era of the Holy Spirit (Rv 20:1-6).

The upcoming Reign of God the Father is about the Almighty being *with and in* all His children on earth, who in turn will become and serve fully living temples for the living God, living directly in the Triune God. The Reign of the Father is the Triumph of the Father's Divine Heart, together with the Triumph of the Sacred Heart of Jesus and the Immaculate Heart of Mary, in and through the Heart of the Holy Trinity. It is the forthcoming fulfillment of our ongoing plea to our Father of, "Thy Kingdom come, Thy Will be done on earth, as it is in Heaven" (Mt 6:10). Such fulfillment, soon to ensue, will bring upon the earth the heavenly Peace, Love, Joy and Happiness for all men of goodwill (Lk 2:14), as we start living in the beginning of the fullness of our inheritance (Paul VI, 1964), in that intermediate time period of tremendous holiness (Rv 20:1-6), before the final unleashing of Satan and his minions (Rv 20:7-10) and the arrival of the literal end of the world and Last Judgment (Rv 20:11-15).

REFERENCES

Apostolate of the Divine Heart. (2012). *Devotion to the Divine Heart of God the Father* (3rd rev. ed.). East Longmeadow, MA: Author.

Bartolo-Abela, M. (2011). *God's gift to humanity: The relationship between Phinehas and consecration to God the Father.* East Longmeadow, MA: Apostolate of the Divine Heart.

Catechism of the Catholic Church. (1993). Vatican City: Libreria Editrice Vaticana.

Congregation for the Doctrine of the Faith. (2000). *The message of Fatima: Third part of the "secret" and translation.* Available at http://www.vatican.va/roman_curia/congregations/cfaith/documents/rc_con_cfaith_doc_20000626_message-fatima_en.html

Lossky, V. (1997). The Divine Light. In *The mystical theology of the Eastern Church.* Yonkers, NY: St Vladimir's Seminary Press.

Paul VI. (1964). *Lumen Gentium.* Available at http://www.vatican.va/archive/hist_councils/ii_vatican_council/documents/vat-ii_const_19641121_lumen-gentium_en.html

Petrisko, T. W. (2002). *The miracle of the illumination of all consciences.* McKees Rocks, PA: St Andrews Productions.

Piccarreta, L. (1899-1938/2007). *The Kingdom of the Divine fiat in the midst of creatures – Book of Heaven: the call of the creature to return to the order, to the place, and to the purpose for which it was created by God* (Vols. 1-36). Miami Beach, FL: DivineWill.cc

Pius XII. (1954). *Ad Caeli Reginam.* Available at http://www.vatican.va/holy_father/pius_xii/encyclicals/documents/hf_p-xii_enc_11101954_ad-caeli-reginam_en.html

St Andrews Productions. (2009). *Seeing with the eyes of the soul: Revelations from God the Father to all mankind.* McKees Rocks, PA: Author.

Contact Information

Apostolate of the Divine Heart
P. O. Box 37, East Longmeadow, MA 01028, USA
Email: adivheart@gmail.com
http://divineheartofgod.wordpress.com

14512413R00056

Made in the USA
Charleston, SC
15 September 2012